Amanda J. Metcalf

Evgenii Shvarts and his Fairy-Tales for Adults

BIRMINGHAM SLAVONIC MONOGRAPHS

Editorial Board

BIRMINGHAM SLAVONIC MONOGRAPHS NO. 8

Amanda J. Metcalf

EVGENII SHVARTS

AND HIS FAIRY-TALES FOR ADULTS

Published by the Department of Russian Language & Literature
University of Birmingham
P.O. Box 363
Birmingham B15   2TT

©   Amanda J. Metcalf 1979

ISBN 0 7044 0350 1
ISSN 0141-3805

Note

An asterisk marks items in the footnotes which have not been individually included in the bibliography. Some are from the archive files listed; the others are mainly short anonymous notes from the 'theatre news' pages of various journals.

The following abbreviations are used to indicate Shvarts's plays cited in the text with page references.

AH	*The Adventures of Hohenstaufen*	Priklyucheniya Gogenshtaufena, *Zvezda*, 1934, no. 11, 43-88
D	*The Dragon*	E. Shvarts, *P'esy*, L., 1962, 311-84
NK	*The Naked King*	ibid., 89-166
OM	*The Ordinary Miracle*	ibid., 435-508
S	*The Shadow*	ibid., 233-310
TYC	*The Tale of a Young Couple*	ibid., 509-78

ALS   *Andersen's Longer Stories*, trans. Jean Hersholt, New York, 1948.

Evgenii L'vovich Shvarts was a doctor's son, born in southern Russia in 1896. During the First World War, the Revolution and the subsequent Civil War he was a student, first in Moscow and then in Rostov-on-Don, where he joined an amateur theatre troupe. In 1921 he went with them to Leningrad (then Petrograd), where the troupe soon broke up and dispersed. Shvarts himself, although not yet a writer, soon became a very welcome addition to the writers' community of the House of the Arts, and a friend of literary groups such as the 'Serapion Brothers' and the 'Oberiu', who appreciated his ability with words.

In 1922, Shvarts went to the Donbass on a visit to his parents and remained there for a year, working on the staff of a miners' newspaper and its associated journal. On his return to Leningrad, he began working in the children's department of the State Publishing House. Here, as one of the editorial board for children's magazines, he became interested in children's literature, and in the late twenties he began to write plays for children - both ordinary adventure stories and, later, adaptations of fairy-tales. In 1931 he left the Publishing House and concentrated on writing plays, both for children and for adults, although until 1940 none of the latter reached the stage.

Throughout the thirties, forties and fifties, Shvarts produced a large number of works for stage, screen, puppet theatre, music-hall and even the circus. His output varied somewhat with changing conditions in the literary world between 1929 and 1958, and his plays have had fluctuating fortunes since his death. Unfortunately, although he had been in the literary environment since the early twenties, his relatively late entry into the theatre meant that he missed the most creative decade of the Soviet period, the twenties, when all kinds of experiments were being tried in the literary, and particularly the theatrical, field. However, echoes of the twenties carried over into his later writing, as a reminder that, no matter how little their respective creative periods overlapped, Shvarts was nonetheless a contemporary of Mayakovskii.

One of the most characteristic features of Shvarts's fairy-tale plays is the use made of what has been referred to as 'fairy-tale logic', which should perhaps be defined at this point (1). Shvarts's construction of fairy-tales is made on the basis of existing themes and motifs, if not actual plots, adapted and reassessed in the light of a particular kind of 'logic', which has its origins in Shvarts's attitude to language. He liked to play with words - twisting them into puns, taking idioms literally, reviving old meanings unexpectedly - and from this comes much of the humour of his plays. This same attitude, applied to the world of the fairy-tale, produces the various forms of 'fairy-tale logic'. One of the most obvious consists in taking a fairy-tale cliché, usually used unthinkingly, and bringing it to life by adapting its literal meaning to suit the demands of the plot. Another method is to take an everyday phrase and put it into the mouth of a fairy-tale character, making the necessary alterations to suit it to its new context. In fairy-tales it is also possible not only to give a lit- eral meaning to puns and idioms, but also to express this in concrete terms. The normal reaction provoked by 'fairy-tale logic' is laughter, combined with surprise that such a logical aspect of the situation had not been thought of before.

Shvarts's fairy-tales, whether for adults or child- ren, are distinguished by their vivid characterisation and dialogue. However 'unreal' the setting, there are no 'unreal' characters - all live and act in a perfectly rational manner, although the logic governing their actions may be of the fairy-tale variety. The development of the plot is always carried out in a highly imaginative way, with a proliferation of new characters and situations emerging to illustrate various points. This trait some- times leads to difficulties in the final act, when the various strands have to be tied together into a conclusion, and the relative weakness of the third act is frequently mentioned in criticisms of Shvarts's work. However, his

---

1. The term 'fairy-tale logic' has been used by (amongst others) N.A. Rabinyants in the chapter on children's drama in S.V. Vladimirov and G.A. Lapkina, eds., *Ocherki istorii russkoi sovetskoi dramaturgii*, II, 1934-1945, L., 1966, 372.

plays are still among the best works in the history of
Soviet drama.

Apart from the quality of the plays themselves, one
of the most interesting features of Shvarts's work is its
place in the convoluted history of Soviet theatre.
Shvarts and his plays survived the worst repressions of
the Stalinist period and saw the beginnings of the post-
Stalin Thaw. The writer died just as he was coming back
into favour after a period of relative silence, but many
of his plays continue to enjoy considerable popularity,
with audiences, if not with those in authority.

This work is intended as a study of Shvarts's
fairy-tales for adults, not only in their literary context, but also in the light of the critical reactions to
them, and the political and literary manoeuvres of the
Soviet period. Since most Soviet works are best examined
in their social context, even in the literary study of
the plays it is worth paying attention to the themes
employed, the specific targets chosen for ridicule, the
external stimuli for the writing of the plays and other
extra-literary aspects.

Evgenii Shvarts holds a very interesting place in
the history of Soviet theatre. He is not the only writer
to have served both the children's and the adult theatre
(although it is noteworthy that only the better writers,
such as Shvarts, Kataev, Rozov and Olesha, can do so
successfully), nor was he the only writer of good fairy-
tales for children. However, he was the only one to use
the genre of fairy-tale plays for adults, and this alone
is sufficient to distinguish him from his contemporaries.

Shvarts is generally assumed to have been exclusively a children's writer until his 'first' play for
adults, The Naked King (Golyi korol'), was written in
1934. In fact he had been involved with the adult
theatre for some time before that. As early as November
1930, even before he left the State Publishing House to
devote himself to writing, he had been one of the writers
from whom had been commissioned 'sketches on topical
themes' for the Leningrad Music-hall's 1931 programme (2).

Shvarts's first full-length play for adults was a
three-act comedy called The Telephone Receiver (Telefon-
naya trubka), which was accepted for production by
Leningrad's Gor'kii Drama Theatre in April 1932. According to one notice the theme of the play was 'time-serving

2. 'Za desyat' dnei', Rabochii i teatr, 1930, no. 64-65, 16.*

as one of the most dangerous forms of disguise for class
enemies' (3). This was the only mention of the play as a
potential production, but it was not subsequently forgotten as a play. A brief résumé of the plot was given by
M. Yankovskii (4). According to him '*The Telephone
Receiver* is about alien elements in the Soviet system'.
While the director of an institute is ill, some of the
staff go into his office to find and alter his reports on
themselves, but they do not realise that the telephone in
the office is off the hook, and that the director is
(somewhat fortuitously) listening in through the telephone
at his hospital bedside. Thus, their behaviour becomes
known and they are exposed to all kinds of ridicule, even
to the point of being made the subject of a music-hall
song - a punishment even more effective than merely losing
their jobs.

According to S. Tsimbal, the play was supposed to be
a realistic comedy, but nonetheless 'Shvarts was *forced* to
resort to fantasy' (5). The italics are mine, since I
think it was more a matter of inclination, and indeed
nature. *The Telephone Receiver*, in fact, is a blend of
outward reality and inner ambiguity. Although the basic
premise - the overheard conversation - is quite possible,
it is also at the least fortuitous, which would be pain-
fully conspicuous in an otherwise totally realistic play.
On the other hand, in the context of some of the other
elements (Shvarts's own individual use of language, and
the ending, with the director's reproaches being passed
all around the town) which begin to lean towards caricature and fantasy, the incident of the receiver becomes
part of a more homogeneous whole. This is why later
commentators, with hindsight, have had no hesitation in
adding the play to the list of Shvarts's fairy-tales.

Yankovskii, writing after the production of the
later play *The Shadow (Ten')*, said, '*The Telephone Receiver*
calls itself just a comedy, but it is just as much a
fairy-tale as *The Shadow*' (6), while Tsimbal, in 1955,
also referred to it as a 'fairy-tale play' into which
'Shvarts boldly introduces elements of satire' (7). Once

3. 'Za desyat' dnei', *Rabochii i teatr*, 1932, no. 11, 16.*

4. 'Detskaya dramaturgiya Leningrada', *Teatr i dramaturgiya*, 1936,
no. 9, 537.

5. S. Tsimbal, 'Evgenii Shvarts i ego skazki dlya teatra', in
E. Shvarts, *Ten' (K postanovke p'esy v Leningradskom Gosudarstvennom
Teatre komedii)*, L., 1940, 10.

6. 'Fantaziya i deistvitel'nost'. O tvorchestve Evg. Shvartsa',
Iskusstvo i zhizn', 1940, no. 2, 14.

7. 'Evgenii L'vovich Shvarts (K 60-letiyu so dnya rozhdeniya)', in
Voprosy detskoi literatury, M., 1955, 416.

again, he is a little wide of the mark, since it seems more appropriate to call the play a 'satire with fairy-tale elements', or better still, 'elements of improbability'.

The next two plays for adults were *The Adventures/ Escapades of Hohenstaufen (Priklyucheniya/Pokhozhdeniya Gogenshtaufena)* - both titles used impartially by a variety of critics - and *The Princess and the Swineherd (Printsessa i svinopas)*, now *The Naked King*. There seems to be a certain amount of confusion with respect to these two, as to which play was written when, and for whom.

Many recent writers, when composing a brief account of Shvarts's life and work, state that *The Naked King* was written in 1934 for Akimov's 'Experimental Workshop' and, if they mention *The Adventures of Hohenstaufen* at all, speak of it as a play which was published in the journal *Zvezda* in November 1934 but had no history other than that. This apparent unanimity is presumably due to the fact that these writers have all read Akimov's contribution to the book *My znali Evgeniya Shvartsa*, a collection of memoirs about Shvarts published in 1966. In this book, Akimov's version of the thirty-year-old events is that he met Shvarts in Moscow in 1931, when Akimov was working with the Vakhtangov Theatre:

> I was told once after a rehearsal that that evening the Leningrad playwright Shvarts was to read his new play ... Shvarts read out *The Adventures of Hohenstaufen*. After a lively discussion, the play was pronounced to be interesting, but in need of polishing. The author ... agreed with all the comments, and never again returned to this work (8).

Concerning *The Naked King*, Akimov's account is:

> When, two years later [i.e. 1933], I was organising an experimental studio of the Leningrad Music-hall, I turned in my search for a repertoire to three dramatists: Shakespeare, Labiche and Shvarts. From the first, I chose *Twelfth Night*, from the second - *Doit-on le dire?* ... Shvarts offered to do a free adaptation of Andersen's fairy-tales, combining 'The Princess and the Swineherd' with 'The Emperor's New Clothes'.

8. In *My znali Evgeniya Shvartsa*, L., 1966, 177.

On that occasion, I had the play almost half-prepared for the stage, but it was forbidden by the Chief Repertoire Committee, for unspecified reasons (9).

In *My znali Evgeniya Shvartsa*, as is usual with memoirs, allowances must be made for varying degrees of inaccuracy, and in this case the accuracy is particularly questionable. With regard to *The Adventures of Hohenstaufen*, Akimov gives the impression not only that the play ceased to exist in 1931, but also that he himself had nothing to do with it after the reading. As will be shown later, this is extremely misleading. As for *The Naked King*, evidence from the 'theatre news' pages of *Rabochii i teatr* between 1933 and 1936 points to its having been written, not for the 'Experimental Workshop' at all, but for the Comedy Theatre. Support for this view is also available from more recent sources. Moreover, M. Yankovskii in 1968 mentioned *The Adventures of Hohenstaufen* in connection with the 'Experimental Workshop' (10). Mark Etkind refers to Akimov's involvement with the Music-hall Workshop, and the fact that the latter closed down in 1934, and then states that 'in 1935 Akimov tried to stage the play *The Princess and the Swineherd*', although without mentioning for which theatre (11).

The Experimental Workshop of the Leningrad Music-hall began work on 1 September 1933 and consisted of twenty-two young and enthusiastic artists from the fields of drama, circus and variety. Akimov later described the early days of the Workshop and mentioned that he had succeeded in establishing contact with Shvarts, and that the latter had agreed to write a play on some contemporary theme, 'a play which will respond to the demand for new genres, without being merely "lightweight drama"' (12). That this play was *The Adventures of Hohenstaufen* is established by a paragraph, dated December 1933, noting that one of the plays being worked on was this 'attempt to create a Soviet fairy-tale' (13).

9.   Ibid.

10. *Leningradskii Teatr komedii*, L., 1968, 12.

11. M. Etkind, *N.P. Akimov - khudozhnik*, L., 1960, 69.

12. 'O putyakh myuzik-kholla', *Rabochii i teatr*, 1934, no. 17, 7.

13. 'Novosti iskusstva', *Rabochii i teatr*, 1933, no. 35, 17.*

It seems that Akimov would have liked to begin the Workshop's season with Shvarts's play. 'The main pre-requisite for such a theatre is its own Soviet drama, growing within, together with and for, the theatre' (14). Also, in connection with Shvarts's involvement, he complained that '... experience has shown that this task [writing a play on a contemporary theme] demands considerably more time than we were able to allot: the play we commissioned will now be the theatre's second work' (15).

Before dealing with the history of *The Adventures of Hohenstaufen*, it is appropriate to examine it as a play. The people concerned work in the financial section of a large building organisation, but this is only one of many possible contexts in Soviet society into which the action could be fitted (provided that such a context was a working, rather than a domestic, environment).

The main characters in the play are the hero, Hohenstaufen (Shvarts had been reading German history and the name appealed to him), who is an economist in the building organisation; a vampire called Upyreva (from the Russian *upyr'* - 'vampire'), who holds a senior post in the same institution; and the cleaning-lady Kofeikina, who turns out to be a good fairy, with whom Upyreva has been waging a bitter feud for centuries. There is also Hohenstaufen's fiancée, Marusya, who works as a clerk in the same office, sundry other colleagues and the director of the organisation, who emerges at the end as a *deus ex machina* to reward Hohenstaufen, punish Upyreva and arrange all the final details.

Hohenstaufen is working on a project to streamline the operation of the organisation, and the plot centres around Upyreva's attempt to sabotage the progress of his work by causing a breach between him and Marusya. This she tries to do by an exchange of faked letters between Hohenstaufen and Bryuchkina, the secretary, and by tricking Marusya into a rendezvous with three of the men in the office simultaneously. Hohenstaufen, however, is assisted by Kofeikina, who is a powerful enchantress, despite the fact that her magic works on a strict quota system - in each quarter she is allowed three major miracles, three transformations and the granting of three wishes ('Smaller miracles, of course, are extras - on petty cash' (*AH*, 51) (16). Upyreva is a real vampire, occasionally reduced to drinking hematogen when she cannot get human blood, and described by Kofeikina as 'the primeval ancestor of bureaucrats ' (*AH*, 53).

14.   'O putyakh myuzik-kholla', *Rabochii i teatr*, 1934, no. 17, 7.

15.   Ibid.

16.   See Note, p. v.

The action of the play is very lively, even the
early expositional scenes being accompanied by various
'magic' effects. There is a very confused scene in the
park - full of awkward situations, chance encounters and
impressive demonstrations of magic - followed by a chase
through the air (Upyreva kidnaps Marusya and the others
set off in pursuit), which ends in the garden of the
director's house by the sea. The ending, however, is
nothing so obvious as a full defeat of Upyreva, since
she manages somehow to vanish from the room in which she
is being held, and immediately multiplies herself into
many different people (all with revealing names such as
Upyrenko, Upyrevich, Vampir and Krovososova - further
variations on the same theme), all with the same attitudes
as herself. The play ends with Kofeikina voicing a
resolution to kill Upyreva 'gradually':

> It will be a good fight. When she says one
> angry word, we will say ten cheerful ones.
> When she upsets people, we will cheer them
> up. She brings dust, cobwebs and dirt, while
> we bring cleanliness, beauty and brightness.
> She puts rust on the pipes and locks on the
> doors, but we set green leaves in the workshops
> and flowers on the tables, in the town squares
> and on the walls. We bring books, theatres,
> science and music. (*AH*, 88)

On this note, Kofeikina and her friend, the warlike old
lady Boibabchenko, leave to continue the fight.

The most remarkable aspect of this play is the way
in which the reality and fantasy, the fairy-tale world
and the scientific world are mixed. In *The Telephone
Receiver* and also in Shvarts's plays for children up till
this point, there had been little more than a highly
imaginative treatment of reality, with the addition, in
The Telephone Receiver, of an element of caricature. It
was in *The Adventures of Hohenstaufen* that the fantastic
took over a really vital role in the action of the play.
Indeed it may have been while he was contemplating writing
this play that Shvarts made the comment:

> After all, one could, for example, just put the
> old witch in the kitchen onto a broomstick and
> have her fly up the chimney. Why not? The
> classical writers weren't afraid to do it.
> Gogol' wasn't afraid. Neither was Hoffmann.
> Andersen took all kinds of liberties ... (17)

17.   Slonimskii, in *My znali Evgeniya Shvartsa*, 11.

In *The Adventures of Hohenstaufen* the irruption of fairy-tale characters and situations into the real world is sudden and startling. But although it is neither wholly realistic nor as wholeheartedly fantastic as his later fairy-tales, nonetheless this play is not merely a halfway stage between realism and fairy-tale. It is a different type of work altogether, for a play in which ordinary people are confronted by extraordinary situations holds possibilities completely different from those of a play in which the people themselves are extraordinary. There is always an element of humour in people who have been placed completely out of context - as in Bulgakov's *Ivan Vasil'evich* (written a little later than Shvarts's play), where the sight of the Soviet petty official, thrust unwillingly into the role of Ivan the Terrible, is just as ridiculous as that of Ivan himself, applying the methods and attitudes of a sixteenth-century autocrat to life in a Soviet block of flats.

To a lesser extent this same element is present in Shvarts's play. There is not a lot of emphasis given to people's attempts to adapt to the unexpected situation of finding themselves involved in a feud between a vampire and a fairy, since attention is concentrated on the feud itself. However, there are instances, such as Boibabchenko's angry reaction to Upyreva's evil plots. The old lady wants to shout abuse to relieve her feelings, but there is nothing in her vocabulary to suit the situation and she is forced to fall back on the typical forms of abuse in the normal Soviet context: 'Why don't you go by car then! No, that's not right. I've got a child at home, too, but *I* don't push in ahead of the queue! That's wrong too. The tram isn't made of rubber, you idiot!' (*AH*, 65)

On the other hand, an equally important element is people's *failure* to be disoriented by strange happenings. This again is not a feature of the later plays, since no one in the fairy-tale world is expected to be surprised by magic happenings. However, it makes a particularly comic impression here, when one sees minor characters taking the magic for granted, especially in the scene when Kofeikina and her friends are flying in pursuit of Upyreva and Marusya. On the way, they meet several people who have seen the fugitives, but who are apparently not in the least discomposed by the sight of an aerial chase undertaken without aeroplanes. First, there is the young man on the roof in his underwear mending his wireless aerial, which Upyreva had broken in passing: he is merely angry. Second, there is the fireman who observes contentedly that he has had a very interesting night watch: 'People keep flying past all the time ...' Finally, there is the worker on the water tower who exclaims: 'Comrades, I've already told you, you're not allowed to fly near the tower! Oh, it's a new lot' (*AH*, 81).

An important question with such mixed reality/
fantasy plays is always whether or not there is to be a
rational explanation. The most commonly used 'rational
explanation' is, of course, the dream, with the hero
waking up at the end to find everything back to normal.
This is the device used by Bulgakov in *Ivan Vasil'evich*;
a safe method to forestall criticism in the early days of
socialist realism. Shvarts, however, seems to have
decided against such a course, although, bearing in mind
the early scene of Hohenstaufen working late at night in
his office, it would have been easy to have made him wake
up in the last act and find that he had been asleep over
his calculations. There is even some support for this
expectation in the text itself. Hohenstaufen, startled
by Kofeikina's first demonstration of magic, exclaims
'What a strange story!' to which Kofeikina rejoins 'It's
not a story, it's a fairy-tale. Go to sleep.' Later,
the magic breaks loose again, he asks what is happening,
and is told 'It's a dream' (*AH*, 59). However, this
potentially rational explanation, perhaps produced for
the benefit of those who might expect such a solution, is
never followed up. There is no final awakening for
Hohenstaufen. At the same time, Shvarts has taken steps
to avoid a too-open declaration of magic. As a result,
there is a deliberate ambiguity about *The Adventures of
Hohenstaufen*, which is perhaps the most intriguing aspect
of the play.

The ambiguity is built up as early as the first
scene, when what has been a quiet chat between two old
ladies about their mutual acquaintance Hohenstaufen takes
on a more mysterious turn as Kofeikina begins to hint at
her magic powers and soon makes a full confession of them
to Boibabchenko. During this scene, a bright flash of
light startles the old lady, but Kofeikina reassures her:
'Don't jump! It was only a tramcar hitting the wire.
After all, it's not midnight yet' (*AH*, 47). Thus, the
force of the 'rational explanation' is somewhat lessened
by the final cryptic statement. After twelve, apparently,
anything might happen. Later, when Kofeikina confesses
and demonstrates her powers to Hohenstaufen, she explains
them with the phrase 'I just have a lot of energy' (*AH*, 49).
To Hohenstaufen's natural protest: 'But fairies don't
exist!' Kofeikina replies that, although this is generally
true, yet there is and always has been one - herself, and
Boibabchenko adds to this a comfortingly 'logical'
generalisation:

And that's the same as if they didn't exist!
How many millions of people there are, have
been and will be - compared with that terrific

number, one single fairy doesn't really
count at all. You could say that, in
general, there aren't any (*AH*, 50).

This deliberate lack of commitment in either
direction continues throughout the play. The magic
element certainly becomes more firmly established in the
later stages, but it is usually referred to in terms of
Kofeikina's boundless 'energy' (a suitable equation for
a country which was making almost miraculous progress by
the application of various types of energy). The idea is
best summed up by the director, who tells her: 'You are
full of the greatest kind of creative energy, which
occasionally produces the impression of a miracle' (*AH*,
84). This channelled use of energy is, in itself, almost
a 'rational explanation' for many of the things that
happen, as when Kofeikina persuades Hohenstaufen to go
home from the office and let her finish his calculations
for him, using her energy working through the machines.
As she says, 'It isn't even a miracle - it's pure science.
They steer boats from the shore, so I will be working
your machines as I go. It's all very simple. Pure
science' (*AH*, 58).

In this play, the word 'science' is not infrequently
used in connection with the phrase 'fairy-tale', almost
in justification of it. Boibabchenko's proof to Hohenstaufen of the truth of Kofeikina's claim is that she
has had the fairy's blood analysed by a doctor: 'And at
the bottom [of the paper] there's the diagnosis. "A
fairy". You see, you can't fight science. It's all very
simple. There's nothing metaphorical about it - it's a
fairy-tale, that's all' (*AH*, 50).

This paradox of using science to prove the existence of a fairy-tale is typical of the whole tone of the
play. Part of the central scene in the park, with its
mixture of magic, farce and drama, relies on purely
'scientific' (if utterly fantastic) happenings. For
example, the hostile crowd which gathers towards the end
of the scene is neutralised by the playing of a flute
which makes them dance. This, of course, is an old theme
in folklore, but also, as Kofeikina explains: 'If you
have jollity and dancing there's no room for anger. It's
a purely scientific miracle. A certain combination of
sounds acts on the motive centres of the brain' (*AH*, 79).

Despite the emphasis on the magic elements, however,
The Adventures of Hohenstaufen is, like the rest of
Shvarts's work, a play with a definite point. The magic
intensifies the conflict, but the conflict remains a
contemporary Soviet one - that of good and bad attitudes
to one's work and fellow workers. In Shvarts's later
fairy-tale plays he continually makes comments on aspects

of contemporary life, but in this play, with its realistic
base, he could make such comments directly. This is his
only play for adults where such a combination of fantasy
and reality is found.

The ultimate evil in the play is Upyreva herself.
The fact that she is a vampire is of relevance only in so
far as it puts her in the same supernatural class as
Kofeikina. Her influence is felt mainly on the human
plane. As Kofeikina says: 'She works on the level where
it is most difficult to catch her out - everyday life'
(AH, 51). Her methods are those of the ordinary unco-
operative bureaucrat, with the same unproductive results.
But, however unacceptable her ways, Upyreva and her kind
are hard to displace. Boibabchenko suggests: 'Let's get
hold of her dossier and prove it all [to the director]',
to which Kofeikina retorts 'Oh, you innocent! The dossier
of a real class enemy is always in perfect order' (AH, 46).

Although Upyreva is the focal point of the attack,
she herself is not a particular target for satire - the
ridicule is directed mainly at her colleagues, other
workers in the organisation with the same characteristics.
These people are cynical, negligent, more interested in
figures than in people, and as such are ideal for
Upyreva's aims.

Despite the untypical nature of the theme and treatment of The Adventures of Hohenstaufen, nevertheless it
shows some concepts and stylistic features which can be
found in many of Shvarts's later works and are essential
parts of his particular creative method. For example, he
has his own individual form of logic, which is displayed
in such cases as Boibabchenko's 'proof' of the political
reliability of the 'new old women' on the grounds that
they never permit themselves to indulge in such irrespons-
ibilities as hooliganism, jumping off moving trams and so
on. The play also contains several specimens of true
'fairy-tale logic', as for example the vacuum cleaner on
which Kofeikina rides, explaining, 'When I was younger I
rode on a broom. Now I'm older and heavier, I ride on a
vacuum cleaner. After all, it is electrical energy' (AH,
58). That last part is very topical in the context of
the drive for electrification in the early years of Soviet
Russia.

Besides the particularly Shvartsian use of logic,
the play also contains early evidence of his distinctive
use of language, one of the features of which is word-
plays; the technique is similar to that involved in
'fairy-tale logic', only on a smaller scale. For example,
Boibabchenko's reaction when Kofeikina drops fifty years
from her age in preparation for the battle with Upyreva,

is: 'I think it's digusting to see an old woman making herself look younger' (*AH*, 73); an expression in common use, but never quite so literally intended.

One other feature, which is echoed in many of Shvarts's later plays, concerns Upyreva. She has one soliloquy in the park, consisting of only one line: 'You make your plans, but I destroy them. You make, and I destroy' (*AH*, 74). This statement voices a theme that is to recur several times in Shvarts's later plays, namely that the power of the evil characters is a negative one, used only to destroy and ruin, while the power of the good characters is positive and constructive. Implicit in this is the belief that, since destruction is a finite process, while construction is potentially infinite, good must ultimately triumph. As Shvarts himself put it, in one of his rare articles: 'He who creates, he who works, will conquer any destructive force - this is the unshakeable law of life' (18).

The Adventures of Hohenstaufen was never actually staged before an audience. It would be a difficult play to produce, with its magic effects, involving flights through the air, transformations into various animals and other technical problems. There are also some faults in its composition, namely one or two inconsistencies of time and place, rather too long and confused a chain of improbable and unexpected events, and - Shvarts's besetting sin - a tendency to try to include all the good ideas provided by his very fertile imagination. The result is a play which, although not yet up to Shvarts's best standard, is based on a good idea, and treated in a delightfully original way, with some very funny moments. It is unique in that this was the only play for adults in which Shvarts used this particular combination of fantasy and reality, and yet in matters of style, method and theme it is in many ways eminently typical.

While still being worked on in the theatre, *The Adventures of Hohenstaufen* seems to have undergone a second reading. It may, in fact, have been the first, as the 1931 reading mentioned by Akimov may have been of *The Telephone Receiver*. This not only is more likely, in view of the chronology of the two plays, but would also explain why Akimov dismissed the further development of the 1931 play so lightly, since he was still in Moscow during the short time when *The Telephone Receiver* was being worked on in Leningrad.

18.   'Tri chuda', *Neva*, 1955, no. 2, 168.

The 1934 reading of *The Adventures of Hohenstaufen* is said to have taken place in the flat of Akimov's friend A.A. Krolenko (then head of the 'Akademiya' publishing house) on 18 June 1934 (19). Yu. Alyanskii quotes a lengthy passage from Krolenko's 'chronicle' (which I was unable to trace to its source) on the subject of this reading. Krolenko apparently had several reservations about the play ('[it] did not get through to me, and I did not understand what the author was trying to say'), but noted that Akimov,

> while agreeing that the composition and some of the characters were unsuccessful, considers the idea of a topical fairy-tale very interesting and sees in it some very tempting material for a synthetic production which he is trying to put on the stage ... He feels that just such a dramatist can help him to realise his new theatrical ambitions.(20)

Meanwhile, work was still continuing on the production in the Music-hall Workshop. The play was mentioned again in *Rabochii i teatr* at the end of August, this time in rather more detail. In a section dealing with prospective productions in the coming season, *The Adventures of Hohenstaufen* was mentioned as the Workshop's second new work for its second season, and due for its première in March 1935. Apparently some obstacles, possibly of a technical nature, were encountered, since the play, originally intended for the 1933-34 season, was now destined for the middle of the 1934-35 one. The production was here described again as an 'attempt to create a Soviet fairy-tale', and the theme is stated as 'the struggle for a new way of life, for new personal relationships and for a new state of mind for socialist man' (21).

This is the last reference to *The Adventures of Hohenstaufen* as a prospective production; the Experimental Workshop closed down before the end of the year. The only explanation offered for this appears to be Akimov's; in a short autobiography he writes that '... at this point the director's mood changed; he got tired of experimenting and closed down our studio' (22). Subsequent references in books and articles look back to the failure of the attempted production.

19. Yu. Alyanskii, 'Obyknovennyi volshebnik', in his *Teatral'nye legendy*, M., 1973, 293.

20. Ibid.

21. 'Chto my uvidim v novom sezone', *Rabochii i teatr*, 1934, no. 24, 7.*

22. N. Akimov, 'Otryvki iz nenapisannoi avtobiografii', in his *O teatre*, L., 1962, 338.

The first such reference, by Akimov in July 1935, began boldly 'What should Soviet comedy be like? This is a question to which there can be no answer'. (It was also a question which many critics were 'answering' with a great assumption of authority at just that time.) Akimov then went on to examine the respective possibilities of various different comic genres, including that of the 'fantastic comedy'.

> The fantastic comedy, which is of enormous interest to the comic theatre, is almost completely neglected by our dramatists! One can point to the interesting experiment *The Adventures of Hohenstaufen* by Evgenii Shvarts. The slight deficiencies of this play are due once again to underestimation and ignorance of all the conditions of this difficult genre. (23)

Akimov is perhaps referring here to the unrestrained nature of the fantastic elements in the play, which lead the action in too many different directions before bringing it to a conclusion. In *The Adventures of Hohenstaufen* the fantastic side has taken possession of the author, whereas the author ought to be in full control of the fantastic.

A year later, in September 1936, M. Yankovskii was loosely attaching the stigma of 'formalism' to the play. He maintained that, despite the undeniable humour óf the work, the gap between the fairy-tale elements and the contemporary side was too wide, and that much of the point was thus lost. The play, he said, 'becomes a wittily-turned but completely formalised "kiddies' fairy-tale" for adults' (24). Yankovskii was apparently still of the same mind four years later, when he wrote in *Iskusstvo i zhizn'* that the play 'remains a half-fairy-tale, half-satire – witty, but completely implausible – on irregularities in everyday life' (25).

The reason why *The Adventures of Hohenstaufen* was never performed was that the Experimental Workshop closed before the play was ready for the stage. The fact that the play was *not* ready for the stage, after more than a year in preparation, is probably at least partly due to practical problems, since it has some technically very difficult moments. One critic who drew attention to this

23. N. Akimov, 'Ne budem narushat' uslovii igry', *Rabochii i teatr*, 1935, no. 13, 6.

24. 'Detskaya dramaturgiya Leningrada', 538.

25. 'Fantaziya i deistvitel'nost'', 14.

16

was Evgenii Min. Apropos of *The Adventures of Hohenstaufen*, he pointed out that 'Shvarts does not worry about
so-called production budgets, or stage technology' and
suggested that perhaps the author's attitude was: '"If
you, the producers and actors, succeed in producing the
play - well and good. If not, well, it can't be helped.
If there can be tragedies meant for reading only, then
why not a fairy-tale play of the same type?"' (26)   It
is true that in none of Shvarts's plays is he particularly
concerned to ease the task of the theatre in staging it,
but, although it has been estimated that more than half
his plays never reached the stage, it is doubtful whether
he would have been satisfied with this situation, or content to regard such plays as for reading only (27).

Subsequent opinions of *The Adventures of Hohenstaufen* are unanimous in praising the originality and
humour of the play (28). However, S. Tsimbal in his book on
Shvarts went on to complain of the 'artificiality and
innate triviality of the problem which the dramatist is
dealing with' and considered that 'the play does not rise
above the level of a witty literary parody'. As he
put it, 'throughout the whole play the playwright has
scattered identification marks: Warning! Fairy-tale!'
and this, in his opinion, detracted from the message. He
commented, justifiably, that 'the writer still thought
that the situations in which people find themselves are
more interesting than the people themselves' (29). It is
true that the characterisation is weak. We know little
except that Kofeikina is good and Upyreva is bad, that
Hohenstaufen loves his work, whereas his colleagues do
not, and so on. Shvarts has time only to draw brief
sketches of his characters in a few lines, before the
magic begins and the fantastic-farcical element takes
over.

One interesting view referred to the early plays as
Shvarts's 'search for himself', and then went on to deal
with the contemporaries of *The Adventures of Hohenstaufen*
(30). On this point Golovchiner quoted the first volume

26. 'Sovetskii skazochnik', in *Teatr i zhizn'*. *Sbornik teatral'no-
kriticheskikh statei*, L., 1957, 83.

27. L. Malyugin in *My znali Evgeniya Shvartsa*, 105.

28. For example, S.V. Vladimirov in Vladimirov and Lapkina, *Ocherki
istorii russkoi sovetskoi dramaturgii*, II, L., 1966, 20, 28.
S. Tsimbal, *Evgenii Shvarts: kritiko-biograficheskii ocherk*, L.,
1961, 88-95.

29. *Evgenii Shvarts*, 90, 93, 95.

30. V.E. Golovchiner, 'Put' k skazke E. Shvartsa', *Sbornik trudov
molodykh uchenykh*, Tomsk, 1971, 170.

of *Ocherki istorii russkogo sovetskogo dramaticheskogo teatra*; this compared Shvarts's play with those of Shkvarkin, Finn and Kirshon which dated from the same period as the *publication* of *The Adventures of Hohen- staufen* in the mid-thirties. Such plays were essentially lightweight comedies, precursors of the 'no- conflict theory' which reigned in later years. Golovchiner was of the opinion that such a comparison was unfair to Shvarts's play because 'the conflict which is depicted in the play is very deep and serious' (31). He himself preferred to accept Akimov's date for the reading of the play - 1931, which brings it much closer to Mayakovskii and *The Bath-house (Banya)*. Certainly, whatever the date may have been, although the magic may detract somewhat from the sharpness of the satirical point, there is no reason to suppose that the play was meant to be an innocuous comedy; and *The Adventures of Hohenstaufen* is much more in the idiom of *The Bath-house* and of Zoshchenko's *Dear Comrade (Uvazhaemyi tovarishch)* (1930), than of Shkvarkin's *Someone Else's Child (Chuzhoi rebenok)* (1933) and other mid-thirties 'comedies of manners'. It is noteworthy that the ending, with Kofeikina and Boibabchenko setting off in pursuit of Upyreva to the tune of a martial song, is very reminiscent of the finale of *The Bath-house*. E. Kalmanovskii main- tained that, in all his early plays, 'the dramatist remained faithful to the spirit which prevailed in the twenties - the time of his youth' and with reference to this play at least, the assertion is certainly justi- fied (32).

After the closing of the Experimental Workshop Akimov, although, as he put it, 'full of directorial energy', spent some months designing sets for productions in various theatres until in 1935 the head of the Leningrad theatre administration offered him the chance to experiment with a bad theatre before it was closed down (33). Akimov and his circle of young actors from the Music-hall descended on the Comedy Theatre and, despite opposition from the older members of the existing troupe, succeeded in changing the face of the theatre so radically for the better that there was no longer any talk

31. Ibid.

32. 'E.L. Shvarts', in S.V. Vladimirov, ed., *Ocherki istorii russkoi sovetskoi dramaturgii*, III, 1945-1967, L., 1968, 138.

33. *O teatre*, 338.

of closing it down.

Another legacy of the Music-hall days which came to the Comedy Theatre with Akimov was the contact with Shvarts. He figured in the list of writers mentioned by M. Bredov, the director of the theatre, in June 1935 when he noted that 'we consider it essential to create a group of highly-qualified dramatists, working in close collaboration with the theatre' (34). Others in the list were Lavrenev, Kataev and Olesha, and Bredov prophesied that 'the basic character of their future works will be comedies of everyday life' (35).

Shvarts's first offering, however, hardly complied with this statement. In July it was noted that:

> Evgenii Shvarts has handed in to the theatre his new comedy, *The Princess and the Swineherd*. Constructed on material from Andersen's fairy-tales, it makes skilful use of the facts of contemporary reality, and, in a series of grotesque figures, exposes the 'deeds and heroes' of fascism.(36)

The degree of accuracy of this description can best be established by an examination of the play. *The Naked King* (as *The Princess and the Swineherd* is now known) is a very lighthearted satirical farce put together from three of Hans Andersen's fairy-tales: 'The Emperor's New Clothes', 'The Swineherd' and 'The Princess on the Pea'. Much of the plot of Act I - the meeting between the Princess and the Swineherd, the magic musical kettle, and the displeasure of the King at his daughter's association with a menial - comes from 'The Swineherd'. However, Shvarts's Princess Henrietta is a charming innocent, quite unlike Andersen's ill-mannered brat (who despises the Swineherd until she finds he is really a Prince). Moreover, Shvarts's Swineherd Heinrich is a real one, and he does not cast the Princess off, but falls in love with her, and he and his friend Christian the Weaver resolve to rescue her from her unwilling marriage to the neighbouring King.

34. Bredov in 'Dramaturgi i teatry', *Rabochii i teatr*, 1935, no. 11, 24.*

35. Ibid.

36. 'V leningradskikh teatrakh', *Rabochii i teatr*, 1935, no. 13, 25.*

At this point Shvarts introduces the episode of
the pea under a dozen mattresses, as a test of the
Princess's racial purity by her fiancé's Minister of
Tender Feelings. Act II follows the plot of 'The
Emperor's New Clothes', with Heinrich and Christian in
disguise as the cheating weavers producing imaginary cloth
for the King to wear on his wedding day. However, the
tone of the ending is changed. In Andersen's story, the
Emperor, rendered ridiculous, but still determined to pre-
serve appearances, is left walking on 'more proudly than
ever, as his noblemen held high the train that wasn't
there at all' (37). There is no indication that his dis-
comfiture will be permanent, or that the townspeople are
prepared to carry the matter any further. This, of
course, was insufficient for Shvarts's purposes and he
brought his story to the point where the King and his
court, shamed before the whole town and in terror of a
popular uprising, retreat in disorder, leaving the field
clear for Heinrich to marry the Princess.

Despite its varied origins, the play makes a very
harmonious whole, with none of the inconsistencies which
might have resulted from the merging of three separate
stories. The composite parts are blended without losing
their individual charm, and even gain more from their new
context.

The Naked King was submitted to the Comedy Theatre
in 1935, that is, in the third year of the Nazi regime in
Germany and as Hitler's power was waxing daily. The
situation in Germany at this time was being observed with
interest and alarm all over Europe. Thus, it is hardly
surprising that, having at last turned to the genre of the
comic fantasy, which allowed such wide scope for comment,
Shvarts should write a play featuring the 'deeds and
heroes of fascism', since at that stage the Nazis were
such easy targets for ridicule. All Shvarts had to do to
gain his effect was to reduce the Nazi creed to colloquial
slang and have the King proclaim that 'Our nation is the
best in the world. All the others are no good, but we're
great' (*NK*, 138). Besides this general declaration, many
of the details of Nazism are also dealt with. The question
of sterilisation arises in a conversation between Christian
and the King's valet:

> Valet: Our state is the highest in the world! If
> you express any doubts about that, then,
> regardless of your age ... (whispers in
> his ear)

37. *Andersen's Fairy Tales*, translated by Jean Hersholt, New York,
1942, 83.

> Christian: Impossible!
>
> Valet: Fact. So that you would not be able to
> produce children who might be
> inclined to criticise. (*NK*, 122)

The unreasonable persecution of those unfortunate enough
not to have been born of Aryan stock is satirised in
Christian's answer to the question 'Are you Aryans?' He
replies, in the manner of one asked whether he is a party
member, 'Oh yes, for years now' (*NK*, 122-3). Book-burning
is also dealt with, an example of an action carried to an
absurd extent by people who are executing orders without
understanding them. The cook explains to Heinrich and
Christian how his book, *This is how to cook, gentlemen!*
was burned:

> ... when it became fashionable to burn books in
> the town squares. In the first three days they
> burned all the really dangerous books, but the
> fashion still hung on and they started to burn
> all books indiscriminately. Now there aren't
> any books left at all, and they're burning
> straw. (*NK*, 126)

The atmosphere of a militaristic dictatorship per-
vades the whole court. The Princess complains that
'Here everything is ... militarised. It's like a military
tattoo. The trees in the garden are drawn up in columns.
Even the birds fly in battalions' (*NK*, 147). The ladies-
in-waiting go about in ranks. The soldiers are a caricature of Nazi military might; they are pictured as being
decadent to the point where they will not fight, and are
unreliable in a crisis - an unfortunately inaccurate
description. They will, however, obey the most ridiculous
orders in perfect unison.

Despite the many references to Nazi attitudes and
practices, it is noteworthy that the King does not bear
any very obvious resemblance to the personality of Hitler
(certainly not to judge from Akimov's sketch of several
of the characters for the Comedy Theatre's production,
where the King's appearance is more in the style of
Charles II or Louis XIV (38)). He is, of course, the
moving force behind all the manifestations of Nazism
already referred to, but they are in operation even before
the opening of the play, and we hear of them only through

---

38.   'Eskiz gruppy personazhei k p'ese E. Shvartsa *Printsessa i
svinopas* (ne osushchestvleno)', *Teatr i dramaturgiya*, 1935, no. 7,
facing 8.*

other people. The character of the King, as presented on
the stage, is that of a capricious, querulous, despotic
old man, with no more evil intention than to marry the
unfortunate Princess against her will. In fact, almost
the only occasion when the King appears in a really fasc-
ist light is in his brief, but violent, outburst after
the Minister of Tender Feelings has declared that in his
opinion the Princess is not of royal blood:

> King: Out! Get out, all of you! You've upset
> me! You've insulted me! Off with your
> heads! To the dungeons! I'll sterilise
> you! Get out! Send her away! Send the
> Princess away this minute! Maybe she's
> semitic! Maybe she's hamitic! Go away!
> Get out! (*NK*, 140)

This instance apart, it is difficult to envisage the
King, as shown on stage, as the vicious tyrant he is
reputed to be.

He is, moreover, shown up as a fool in his relations
with his court. The Prime Minister's extravagant flattery,
under its transparent disguise of plain speaking, never
fails to please. The court jester is very popular with
his sovereign for his funny stories of the heavy slapstick
type. The fact that the King laughs uproariously at such
stories is yet another comment on his general level of
intelligence.

The court, although it naturally centres around the
King (as shown by the great commotion which attends the
levee du roi), seems also to have a quite independent
significance of its own. This has the effect of diffusing
the satire over more than one field. We have seen in *The
Adventures of Hohenstaufen* that Shvarts's very fertile
imagination was apt to take control on occasion. This is
perhaps also true of *The Naked King*, where, having set his
parody of a dictator in a royal court, Shvarts could not
resist the temptation to satirise the manners, habits and
conventions of court life, thus diluting the more pointed
anti-Nazi material with some less specific observations on
rigid establishments in general and royal ones in
particular. At the King's court great emphasis is placed
on the ancient and sacred traditions, which tends to draw
attention away from the Nazi target, since the two-year-
old regime must have been the least afflicted by tradition
of all the European systems at that time. The mention of
old-established courts and traditions immediately suggests
the rest of Western Europe as an alternative target for
satire, and in fact in one of the early versions of the
script Henrietta is referred to as 'the daughter of the
King of Switzerland', an additional indication in this

direction (39). Thus, *The Naked King* could be regarded as the precursor of the later play, *The Shadow*, in showing the Nazi threat in the context of Western society.

Humour at the expense of royalty is to be found in the scene where the court scholar traces the Princess's line of descent. The custom of nicknaming kings is exposed to ridicule as the scholar recites the list, from 'Georg I, called, because of his great deeds, Georg the Great' and his son 'Georg II, called, because of his great deeds, Georg the Ordinary', through 'Wilhelm I (the Merry) ... Heinrich II (Devil Take Him), Philip I (the Abnormal) ...' and so on, down to the present King, 'Georg XV, called, because of his great deeds, Georg the Bearded' (*NK*, 134-5). The anti-monarchist theme is continued in the national anthem of the land in which, as with the Nazi creed, all the elevated sentiments usually expressed in royalist national anthems are condensed into one couplet, colloquial almost to the point of being inarticulate: 'Look at our King! Isn't he a King! Hey there, say there! What a great King! Hurrah!' (*NK*, 145)

There is also an attack on the rigid etiquette prevalent at royal courts. When the 'weavers' arrive at the court they address themselves in turn to the valet, the cook and the boots, obtaining no reply except from the latter, who asks what they want. From him the message is passed along the line until it reaches the valet, who then condescends to greet the new arrivals. Thus, only after the application has been processed through the proper channels will the man in charge take notice of it. This phenomenon, of course, has a wider relevance than to royal courts, being applicable to all forms of bureaucracy, not least the Soviet system.

There are other even less specific targets for satire, many of them appropriate in almost any context, including a Soviet one. One of these is the court poet, a colleague of all artists who subordinate their art to their material well-being. His main talent lies in requesting favours, and his reaction when ordered to go and report on the progress of the invisible clothes is to say resignedly, 'Well, if it comes to the worst, I'll make something up! And not for the first time either!' (*NK*, 150)

The Minister of Tender Feelings is almost more relevant in a Soviet context than in any other. There were many people who adapted to the Revolution as a matter

39. *'Golyi korol'*. P'esa v 2-kh deistviyakh. Avtograf (otryvki)', TsGALI, fond 2215, opis' 1, ed. khr. 7, list 97.

of expediency, after serving the old regime faithfully, and the Minister is a good example of a man determined to remain on the winning side for his own safety. His response to the unease amongst the party on the dais when the King appears in his wedding 'garments' is to suggest that 'We'd better form a Temporary Committee for the Safety of Courtiers', which is obviously a reference to the Provisional Government established on the Tsar's abdication. However, when the little boy sees the King and suddenly calls out 'But Papa, he's got nothing on!' the Minister loses no time. As the crowd begins to shout he abandons the court party, and rushes away into the palace crying confusedly, 'My mother's a blacksmith, my father's a washerwoman! Down with tyranny!' (*NK*, 164)

Apart from the satire, there is a good deal of pure comedy, and even farce, in *The Naked King*. The first act particularly, which is largely expositional, is fairly straight humour. Act II also, for all its verbal satire, still provides many opportunities for visual comedy, such as the King's descent from his enormously high bed by umbrella-parachute and the antics of the unfortunate courtiers, sent to report on the weavers' progress and shamelessly mocked by Christian, who plays on the fact that they do not know where the cloth is supposed to be or which way up it ought to be held.

The play is rich in verbal comedy as well as visual humour. By contrast with *The Adventures of Hohenstaufen*, *The Naked King*, apart from its fantastic setting, is not a 'magic' play. The singing, talking kettle is represented more as a product of Christian's skill than as something miraculous and the 'magic' cloth is, of course, not magic at all. Thus, there is less scope for the fairy-tale logic which appeared in *The Adventures of Hohenstaufen* and later became such a regular feature of Shvarts's fairy-tale plays. But fairy-tale logic is only word play translated into objects, and there is no shortage of typically Shvartsian language in *The Naked King*.

Shvarts's love of experimentation with words even led him to invent a new language for the Princess's strict German governess, a language full of nonsense words, fragments of German and pseudo-German constructions such as 'Take your hands of your pockets out! It vulgar being is!' (*NK*, 108) Another of his favourite methods was to adapt common Soviet expressions to suit the context. Thus, the usual sarcastic rebuke to people pushing through a crowd, 'Why don't you go by car then!' when used by one of the townspeople in the crowd at the wedding, becomes 'Why don't you drive your own carriage then, if it's too crowded for you here!' (*NK*, 160) Perhaps the best aspect of *The Naked King* is the verbal one. It is a very funny play to read, but if the visual comedy were over-emphasised much of the effect would probably be lost.

As the plans for the new (1935-36) season advanced, *The Princess and the Swineherd* was, in August 1935, designated in *Rabochii i teatr* as the second new work of the Comedy Theatre, to be staged after their production of Louis Verneil's *Ma Crime*. At this point, too, there was a reference to some other play which Shvarts was writing 'on Soviet material' for this theatre (40). This is presumably what Bredov had had in mind in June.

The première of *Ma Crime* was in November 1935, but once again, as in the case of *The Adventures of Hohen-staufen*, something was delaying the Shvarts play; only in February 1936 did *Rabochii i teatr* announce that 'work has begun on the production of a fairy-tale comedy by E. Shvarts, *The Princess and the Swineherd*. The theatre proposes to hold an open rehearsal of the play at the end of this season' (41). Whatever the problem, the play was delayed to such an extent that Shvarts's other new play ('written in the style of a cheerful, entertaining comedy of everyday life, [its theme being] the relation-ships within the family of a scientific worker') had overtaken it and was said to be due for its première at the end of March (42). This latter play remains un-identified, and seems to have met the same fate as *The Princess and the Swineherd*, for neither of them was staged as promised.

Akimov's account, in 1966, of this phase of the play's history was (as quoted above) that the production was halfway to completion when it was banned by the Repertoire Committee 'for unspecified reasons'. Obviously, *The Princess and the Swineherd* was one of the many victims of the general removal of plays of all kinds during 1936, after the formation of the Committee on Artistic Affairs under the chairmanship of P. Kerzhentsev.

An account of the activities of the Committee listed many of the banned productions and noted that 'as was subsequently announced at a conference of artistic

40. 'V leningradskikh teatrakh', *Rabochii i teatr*, 1935, no. 16, 17.*

41. 'V leningradskikh teatrakh', *Rabochii i teatr*, 1936, no. 3, 33.*

42. Ibid.

workers, "out of 19 new productions put on in the 1936-37 season, 10 had to be removed from the repertoire"' (43). This presumably does not take into account those productions which were banned before they even reached the stage, of which *The Princess and the Swineherd* was one.

In view of this, it is hardly surprising that, at a meeting of the board of the Leningrad branch of the Union of Soviet Writers in February 1936, when the question of 'close contact with playwrights' arose, Akimov was moved to complain that 'experience shows that one is forced to put on, not the plays which one has been counting on, but works created without the slightest participation by the theatre' (44). When the time came to sum up the successes of the Comedy Theatre over the 1935-36 season, the four new productions mentioned did not include *The Princess and the Swineherd* (45).

After its disappearance from the plans of the Comedy Theatre, the play was almost completely forgotten for many years owing to the fact that, unlike *The Adventures of Hohenstaufen*, it had never been published. M. Yankovskii mentioned the play along with *The Telephone Receiver* and *The Adventures of Hohenstaufen* in his 1936 article, but four years later dealt only with the other two and *The Shadow* (46). Even S. Tsimbal in his book, although well aware of the existence of *The Naked King* (written, according to him, for the Experimental Workshop), mentioned Shvarts's '*encounter* with Andersen' (my italics) only in connection with the subsequent children's play *The Snow Queen (Snezhnaya koroleva)* (47). He did not mention *The Naked King* until twenty-five pages later.

However, the play was apparently not forgotten by the author, and in the course of Shvarts's sojourn in Kirov, after his evacuation from blockaded Leningrad, he seems to have offered the play to the Kirov Regional Drama Theatre. A mention of this is found in a

43. B. Nazarov, O. Gridneva, 'K voprosu ob otstavanii dramaturgii i teatra', *Voprosy filosofii*, 1956, no. 5, 88.

44. 'Zayavki i p'esy. Na zasedanii pravleniya Leningradskogo Soyuza Sovetskikh Pisatelei', *Rabochii i teatr*, 1936, no. 3, 31.

45. A. Movshenson, 'Dve prem'ery v Teatre komedii', *Rabochii i teatr*, 1936, no. 12, 20.

46. 'Detskaya dramaturgiya Leningrada', 538; cf. 'Fantaziya i deistvitel'nost''.

47. *Evgenii Shvarts*, 132.

recently-published letter from Shvarts to his friend
Malyugin in which he says that 'The work on *The Naked King*
has stopped for the moment. I don't know why' (48).
Apparently the halt was more than temporary, for there is
no evidence that the production ever reached the stage.

The Naked King, when first written, was a new and
unexpected phenomenon in the Soviet theatre of the
thirties. Satire existed, farce existed (although
regarded with some disfavour as an unproductive art form),
musical comedy also existed. But here was a combination
of all these elements where quick-fire verbal humour and
pointed satire alternated with broad slapstick comedy and
cheerful songs and dances, the whole placed in a setting
totally unfamiliar to the Soviet mind. Even *The Adventures
of Hohenstaufen* and Mayakovskii's fantasies had been at
least partially rooted in realism, but not this play. Its
raison d'être, of course, was the satire and in those days
the anti-Nazi element was meant to be the most important.
However, S. Tsimbal in his book on Shvarts took exception
to the treatment of this theme in the play. In his
opinion, Shvarts had been guilty of taking a serious
situation too lightly. 'In *The Naked King* Shvarts had not
yet risen to the level of a [genuine] lampoon and had not
escaped from the bonds of a light, non-committal irony' (49).
This rather too harsh judgement was in its turn criticised
ten years later by V. Golovchiner, who pointed out that at
the time no-one did take Hitler very seriously, and that
the prevailing attitude of Russians to Germany in the early
thirties was an eager anticipation of the day when the
German workers would follow their example and rise in
revolution. Golovchiner thus justified Shvarts's
attitude:

> From this point of view, fascism appeared to
> be a definitely temporary and short-lived
> phenomenon ... Therefore, the 'tolerance' of
> which Tsimbal accuses Shvarts with respect
> to *The Naked King* is a reflection of the
> feelings of the majority of Soviet people
> at the beginning of the thirties. (50)

48. Letter from E. Shvarts to L. Malyugin, 2 March 1943, in 'Iz
perepiski Evgeniya Shvartsa', *Voprosy literatury*, 1977, no. 6,
221-2.

49. *Evgenii Shvarts*, 164.

50. 'Put' k skazke E. Shvartsa', 176.

In fact there is not enough explicitly anti-Nazi
material to carry the play as a political lampoon
against that target alone, and what there is is super-
imposed on, rather than imbedded in, the other components.
Thus the Nazi references can be emphasised or underplayed
at will.

This was the reason for the play's considerable
popularity in the production by the new Moscow theatre,
the Sovremennik, in the sixties, despite the fact that
the play was twenty-five years old and that the Nazi
question had not only shown itself to be no matter for
laughter, but had subsequently been definitively settled,
so the play should therefore have been out of date.
Avril Pyman, in her introduction to three of Shvarts's
plays, says that the Sovremennik production 'was widely
regarded as a wildly successful slapstick parody of the
last years of Stalinism' (51).

For years *The Naked King* had existed only as manu-
scripts and in the typed copies used by the theatres, and
it remained among Shvarts's papers until after his death
when, as A. Shtein reported: 'They found it in [Shvarts's]
writing desk when they were sorting out the archives' (52).
The discovery led to the subsequent production of the play
in 1960. It was an eminently suitable play for such a
theatre as the Sovremennik - '[a theatre] born of the
enthusiasm of the disciples of the Art Theatre Studio
and, to an even greater degree, born of the spirit of the
new times' (53). Moreover, an enthusiastic young theatre
needed to make changes, even from the 'Thaw' plays, with
their newly-acquired freedom of expression. In his
'portrait' of the Sovremennik's director, Efremov, R. Benyash
wrote:

> Feeling the need for a complete switch to a
> new genre, Efremov included in the Sovremennik's
> repertoire Evgenii Shvarts's unfinished fairy-
> tale *The Naked King*. There were different
> reactions to this satirical production of a
> fairy-tale-with-a-message. Some thought it the
> theatre's greatest achievement. Others saw
> inadequacy of design, a lack of the artistry so
> essential in this genre. Both schools of thought,
> however, realised the need for stylistic variety. (54)

51. E. Shvarts, *Three Plays*, Oxford, 1972, xix.

52. A. Shtein, *Povest' o tom, kak voznikayut syuzhety*, M., 1965,
91.

53. Ibid.

54. 'Efremov', in *Portrety rezhisserov*, book 1, M., 1972, 200.

The première of *The Naked King* was on 20 March 1960, during the Sovremennik's tour in Leningrad, and the play ran without a break throughout the sixties. Presumably the run ceased only when E. Evstigneev returned from the Sovremennik to the Art Theatre in the early seventies, since without the King the play could not continue.

Unpublished in the thirties, *The Naked King* has, since 1960, appeared in two of the three editions of the main collection of Shvarts's plays (1960 and 1962) and also in a photocopied version taken from the 1960 edition. Its omission from the 1972 edition of the plays, where its place is taken by the harmless *Little Red Riding Hood (Krasnaya shapochka)*, while the usually less-favoured *The Dragon (Drakon)* remains, is one of the more mystifying aspects of the play's recent history. In the course of the sixties, *The Naked King* was taken on tour by the Sovremennik to places as far apart as Leningrad and Baku, and was also performed in Riga, by the State Theatre of Russian Drama there (the première was on 23 May 1960).

A few years later, in 1963, a film was made called *Cain XVIII (Kain XVIII)* based on *The Naked King*. The story is that of a despot who plans to rule the world by killing all his enemies with the aid of a poisonous mosquito, but is foiled by a young musician who is in love with the princess whom the tyrant wants to marry.

According to Irina Corten, Shvarts had begun working on the scenario just before his death, but it was a half-hearted project and remained unfinished until the playwright N. Erdman completed it after Shvarts's death (55). The film was directed by M. Shapiro and N. Kosheverova and starred Erast Garin (a trio who had worked on Shvarts's film scenarios before). Also featured were current and former actors of the Comedy Theatre such as A. Beniaminov and L. Sukharevskaya. Tsimbal categorised the film as a 'political lampoon, directed against the neo-fascist atom-bomb men and the frenzied lackeys of imperialism' (56). Despite several minor criticisms, some of which were connected with the combination of two individual satirical styles, Tsimbal was of the opinion that the film was generally a success. Indeed, considering the rarity of the 'fairy-tale lampoon' as a film genre, he declared that, 'by virtue of this fact alone,

55. Irina H.S. Corten, 'Evgenij Švarc: Man and artist', Ph.D. thesis, Berkeley, 1972, 45.

56. S. Tsimbal, 'Kainovo tsarstvo', *Iskusstvo kino*, 1963, no. 8, 79.

the production of *Cain XVIII* deserves the most favourable attention' (57).

In the Sovremennik production the play was a satire on dictatorship and megalomania, being performed in the context of the aftermath of Stalinism, and probably many of the thousands of people who saw it or heard of it in the sixties did not realise that it was twenty-five years old. Even to those who did know the play's history, it seemed very appropriate. V. Kardin, summing up the Sovremennik's first decade in 1966, wrote of the *Naked King* production: 'The release of emotions from social and national institutionalism is what attracted the young theatre by its close similarity to our own time' (58). A. Lebedev came even closer to an explicit statement in 1968: 'By means of laughter the human race breaks with its past. It is for this reason that we now laugh so merrily at Shvarts's *The Naked King*' (59). To the Soviet playgoer of the sixties the context of the play was obviously a rigid autocracy of some kind, but with the anti-Nazi elements to a certain extent absorbed in the more general satire and the visual comedy, Stalinism would probably be a more obvious parallel than Nazism. Moreover, such references as those to anti-Semitism and isolationism could equally well apply to the later years of Stalin's rule. Even the reference to the 'ancient and sacred traditions' might now have some relevance to the conventions of forty years of Soviet power, where it could never have applied to the Nazi regime in its second year. Such phenomena as the court poet, the rigid court (or bureaucratic) procedure, and the suppression (if not the actual burning) of books would stand out in the minds of the 1960 generation. Apart from the political aspect, the play was sure to appeal to a public to whom Shvarts was no longer an unknown quantity, and who, after years of socialist realism, were prepared to accord an enthusiastic reception to such an unusual and colourful work.

Apparently, despite the good reception of the Sovremennik production, the preparation had been by no means easy.

> By contrast [with Volodin's *Five Evenings*], the Sovremennik's second 'succès de scandale', *The Naked King*, appeared to evoke relatively

57. Ibid, 80.

58. 'Posle pervogo desyatiletiya', *Teatr*, 1966, no. 4, 18.

59. A. Lebedev, 'Skazka est' skazka', *Teatr*, 1968, no. 4, 44.

> little official comment, though its birth pains
> in the last quarter of 1959 were greater and
> the gossip about it incommensurately more
> insistent (60).

Campbell quoted no sources for these claims, nor did he
give any details, but at the end of the same article he
returned to this theme:

> Perhaps because it has been relatively quiescent,
> the Soviet theatre [since the Thaw] has met with
> not unsympathetic treatment from the authorities.
> It is true that the extent of cuts and changes
> resulting from the preliminary and subsequent
> censorship of plays is unascertainable. It is
> a relevant factor which has operated, for
> example, in relation to the initial production
> of Shvarts's *The Naked King* ... (61)

According to my information, the very fact that the
play's première took place in Leningrad was due to a
cunning political move on the part of the theatre.
Apparently the first 'open rehearsal', attended by the
censors, took place on the eve of the Theatre's departure
for Leningrad, and the play, as a dazzling spectacle of
pure entertainment, was passed without question. The
Leningrad Party authorities under V. Tolstikov might have
been less favourably disposed, but in the face of a
permission signed in Moscow there was little they could
do. By the time the theatre returned to Moscow, the play
was well-established on the stage and its reputation had
long since reached the capital, where audiences were
impatiently awaiting their turn to see it. Thus, although
the play contained several very embarrassing moments for
the authorities, it would have been impossible, at the
height of the 1960 Thaw, to have banned it without
creating an even more embarrassing situation. However,
it is claimed (by someone who saw the Leningrad première
and afterwards compared notes with friends in Moscow) that
several cuts were made over the next few years. Apparently
Furtseva, the Minister of Culture, saw the play several
times, and on each occasion a few more lines were removed.

One of the very first sections to be cut was the
speech by the Minister of Tender Feelings to the effect
that 'since His Highness announced that our nation is the
greatest in the world, we have been ordered to forget
completely all foreign languages' (*NK*, 109). Two similar

60. A.J.C. Campbell, 'Plays and Playwrights', *Survey*, January
1963, 70.

61. Ibid., 76.

speeches were also cut out later: one defending 'our ancient national traditions, sanctified by the creator himself' (*NK*, 122), and the other including the line 'all the others are no good, but we're great' (*NK*, 138). The conversation between the cook and the 'weavers' on the subject of book-burning also proved too relevant for Furtseva, as did some of the King's dialogue with his court scholar about the Princess's ancestry. The scholar begins at the beginning - with Adam, which horrifies the King because 'wasn't Adam a Jew?' This anti-Semitic reference might have been passed as a purely anti-Nazi element - although another, a few pages later, was cut (*NK*, 140) - had it not been for the scholar's comforting assurance that 'I have information that he was a Karaim' (*NK*, 134). The mention of the Karaim (Turkic Jews from the Crimea, who were slightly less underprivileged than other Jews) tied the reference too firmly to a Soviet context, and the conversation was cut. The most ironical cut of all - only a few words - was made in the speech where the King praises his court jester. 'That's what I like about him - it's his pure humour. *None of these allusions and innuendoes ...*' (*NK*, 130)

Not all the barbed lines were cut, however. References to literary hacks, in the person of the court poet, were retained (*NK*, 135, 150) and the Princess's soliloquy complaining about the militarised and tradition-bound court (*NK*, 147) seems to have survived intact. No definite information is available about the Prime Minister's words 'Our whole national system, all our traditions, are held up by unshakeable idiots' (*NK*, 157), although the monologue which contains these lines was certainly retained. What, if any, further cuts were made by the time the play's run finished is unknown, but, with even those few lines missing, a good deal of the effect would be gone.

These three plays, Shvarts's first ventures into the adult theatre, show an interesting progression from reality to fantasy. The mild improbability inherent in *The Telephone Receiver* became the volcanic intrusion of magic into the real world in *The Adventures of Hohenstaufen*, and finally realism was altogether discarded for the first time in *The Naked King*. The three plays also show one common feature - that none of them reached the stage at the time they were written. However, even this period of failure was not without benefit, for it marked the beginning of the long collaboration between Shvarts and Akimov, without which many of Shvarts's plays would not have been written, let alone staged.

After the abortive attempt to stage *The Naked King* in 1935-36, Shvarts devoted the rest of the thirties to writing children's plays - fairy-tales and realistic plays - both for the live and the puppet theatres. From this period date two of his best-known children's fairy-tales: *Little Red Riding Hood* (1936), an adaptation of Perrault which emphasised the power of friendly collective action, and *The Snow Queen* (1938), a rather 'older' fairy-tale, based on Hans Andersen and usually regarded by Russian commentators as Shvarts's best children's play. He also, in 1938, wrote a realistic play on the theme of national defence, called *Our Hospitality (Nashe goste-priimstvo)*, which was to have been performed by the Comedy Theatre, but which met with various obstacles on the way - from the reluctance of the Repertoire Committee to pass a play based on the 'impossible' incident of a foreign plane crossing the Soviet border, to the final insurmountable block of the Ribbentrop-Molotov pact in 1939, which effect-ively put an end to any such work.

Meanwhile, at some point during the years immedi-ately preceding the war, Shvarts wrote what has always been considered one of his best plays - *The Shadow*. It is not known when the play was begun; Akimov merely stated in his memoirs that 'after long hesitation over a subject for a "play for adults"' he had suggested that Shvarts write a new version of Andersen's story, 'The Shadow' (62). According to him, the first act was completed within ten days, while the second and third took months. Since the play was first performed early in 1940, this would put the commencement date at least as far back as 1939. In fact, there is a portrait of Shvarts by Akimov, dated 1938, which shows him standing in a room with a portrait of Andersen on the wall, and a vague shadowy figure in a top hat sitting on a stool in the background, which implies that the original suggestion, at least, was made as early as this. M. Zhezhelenko also mentioned the portrait, although he considered that, at that stage, Shvarts 'was not yet thinking of working on *The Shadow* as a play' (63).

It was with *The Shadow* that the association between Shvarts and Akimov, already of several years' standing, finally produced a visible result after three unsuccessful tries. The play was, from the first, intended for the Comedy Theatre, and was a product as much of Akimov's faith in and persistent support for Shvarts and his work, as of the author himself.

62. Akimov in *My znali Evgeniya Shvartsa*, 177.

63. 'Akimov' in *Portrety rezhisserov*, book 1, 60.

Shvarts's *The Shadow* is based loosely on Hans
Andersen's story 'The Shadow' (Skyggen), written in
1847. Andersen's tale is itself not entirely original,
but takes its theme - the figure of the shadowless man -
from Adelbert Chamisso, whose book *Peter Schlemihls
wundersame Geschichte* (1814) deals with a man who sells
his shadow to the Devil. Nor was Andersen unwilling to
acknowledge the borrowing, for in his own story he wrote:

> What annoyed [the scholar] most was not so much
> the loss of his shadow, but the knowledge that
> there was already a story about a man without
> a shadow. All the people at home knew that
> story. If he went back and told them his
> story, they would say he was just imitating
> the old one.(*ALS*, 53) (64)

However, Andersen was in no danger of such an accusation,
for his tale is by no means mere imitation of Chamisso's
novel. Perhaps the only common ground they have is the
fact that the plots range over several years and several
different settings. Chamisso's Peter Schlemihl sells his
shadow to the 'man in grey', and the rest of the story
concentrates on his life without it, while the shadow itself never reappears after the 'man in grey' has put it in
his pocket. In Andersen's story, however, the Shadow
leaves the Scholar at his request and becomes a separate
being capable, firstly, of persuading its former master to
reverse their roles and, finally, of having him put to
death when he becomes an inconvenience. Andersen's Shadow
marries a princess - having convinced her of his wisdom by
sending the Scholar (as his Shadow) to talk to her ('"What
a man that must be, to have such a wise shadow!" she
thought' (*ALS*, 60). He then executes the unfortunate man
on the night of the wedding, because he had threatened to
disclose the truth to the Princess. Despite its wide range
of time and action, the story contains a minimum of characters - the Scholar, his Shadow, and the Princess who
appears only towards the end.

Shvarts, like Andersen, did not imitate his precursor, but created his work on the basis of the other's
material. In fact, he quotes Andersen's own claim (from
his autobiography) at the head of the play: 'Someone else's
theme became, as it were, a part of my own flesh and blood.
I reworked it, and only then let it out into the world'
(*S*, 235). Moreover, Andersen's story is mentioned in the
play. When the Scholar loses his shadow, the Innkeeper's
daughter, Annunziata, exclaims fearfully 'The man without a

64. Page references from *Andersen's Longer Stories*, translated by
Jean Hersholt, New York, 1948.

shadow - but that's one of the saddest fairy-tales in the world' (*s*, 256). Thus the play may be regarded not as an adaptation, but as a re-enactment of the original conflict in which any outcome is possible.

Shvarts's version takes the theme of Andersen's story and applies it to the contemporary European scene, using it as an indictment of people who are prepared to submit to a shadow. It is this purpose as well as the demands of the theatre which together account for most of the differences between the two works. Shvarts has surrounded the three basic characters with a whole social structure, from the Minister of Finance down to the Inn-keeper's daughter, fixed the action in one place and narrowed the time-span down to a few weeks. Thus the story is lengthened while the plot acquires greater unity of time and place.

The adaptations of the form of the original give rise to some changes and additions to the plot. Shvarts's Princess is present in the story from the beginning. The Scholar meets her first and they fall in love, but the Shadow steals her from him in order to gain the throne. Moreover, the increased number of characters provides material for a much more involved plot, as the court circles carry on complicated intrigues against the Scholar and each other.

The most radical change is in the ending. Andersen's story shows the gradual downfall of the Scholar to such a degree that he gives up his own identity and virtually ceases to exist, long before he is actually executed. Shvarts's play, however, could not possibly have ended thus. It would not have been in keeping either with Soviet convention or with Shvarts's own philosophy.

In Shvarts's play, much more attention is given to the setting. The action takes place in a 'souther land' - somewhat Italian as to appearance and the names of the local inhabitants, but otherwise no ordinary country. This is the land where 'everything that is told in the fairy tales ... happens ... in real life every day' (*s*, 238). Here the fairy-tale characters live, more or less happily ever after, in retirement following the Happy Ending.

One of the most striking features of *The Shadow* is the gallery of such characters presented in the course of the play. As a work, it depends less on dramatic incidents than on the interaction of the various people involved in the plot, and in this way it is one of Shvarts's more sophisticated plays. Certainly, in a study of *The Shadow*, the main interest lies in the characters, and the changes (or lack of change) in their attitudes in the course of the play. Of these characters, the Scholar, the Shadow and the Princess are taken from Andersen; the rest are purely Shvartsian inventions. Even the basic three are more Shvarts's characters than Andersen's.

Shvarts's Scholar is a complete contrast to Andersen's. Both are idealists, but Andersen's hero 'wrote books about those things in the world that are true, that are good and that are beautiful' (*ALS*, 53), whereas the aim of Shvarts's Scholar is 'how to make everyone happy' (*s*, 251) - a much less passive vocation (even though his attitude to the task does seem to be more theoretical than practical). He is handicapped by naiveté and inexperience in the ways of the world, and is therefore very easily deceived by the Shadow. However, when at last he realises the true situation, he sets himself to oppose the Shadow, and refuses to give in, even in the face of death. 'You see, to conquer you have to go on, even to death' (*s*, 307). This seemingly suicidal deter- mination is finally rewarded, for as his head rolls, so does his Shadow's, and the real man must be restored with the Water of Life in order to save the Shadow.

It is interesting that no-one, among either the Soviet or the Western critics, has made any mention of the symbol of the man who is executed and then resurrected. Naturally, none of the play's Soviet supporters would have referred to it, but even in the late forties, when the play was not recalled with approval, the parallel (which could have been used with scathing effect in an attack) did not seem to occur to anyone.

The Shadow is the exact opposite of his former master in every way. As cynical as the Scholar is idealistic, as devious as he is straightforward, as ruthless as he is kindhearted, the Shadow sets out to destroy his master. The prize is the Princess and her throne, but there is also a motive of abstract hatred, an attempt to foil the Scholar for no other reason than that the Shadow represents the negative side of life, the destructive force, essentially opposed to anything as positive as the ideals for which the Scholar stands. There is also the traditional hatred of the slave for the master. However, the Shadow's victory, although comprehensive, is only temporary and, discredited by the untimely loss of his own head and with the court closing in on him menacingly, he vanishes from between the hands of his would-be captors. Like Upyreva in *The Adventures of Hohenstaufen*, he has not gone for ever, and the Scholar looks ahead to other encounters: 'He has gone now, only to cross my path again and again in the future. But I'll recognise him. I'd know him again any- where' (*s*, 308).

The Princess, caught up in the rivalries and intrigues of the court, is an unfortunate orphan. Her royal upbringing has left her disillusioned and distrustful, and it is almost in spite of herself that she falls in love with the Scholar. His sincerity intrigues and attracts her, but she still retains enough of her basic distrust of humanity to believe the Shadow's slanders and, on this basis, to reject the Scholar out of hand. Although her eyes are opened at last by the sight of the Shadow almost grovelling to placate the Scholar, for her there is to be no happy ending, since the Scholar chooses the Innkeeper's daughter, Annunziata, instead.

Annunziata is the only person who is on the side of the Scholar throughout the play. He receives occasional warnings and advice from one or two other characters, but wholehearted support comes only from Annunziata. She helps him because she loves him. Even when he is in love with the Princess, Annunziata stays by him because she believes he is in danger, and she is mildly infuriated by his state of euphoric oblivion. Later, she comforts him when he is near to despair, and in the final act at the palace it is she who answers his appeal for confirmation of his claim that he is the substance and not the shadow. Finally, she has her reward when the Scholar leaves the court to its own devices and takes her with him.

Against the Scholar and Annunziata, and acting in support of (or at least in temporary alliance with) the Shadow, is the elite society of the land. The people surrounding the throne are corrupt, power-seeking and possessed of an inverted system of values. It is a society such that a Shadow can rise to the throne, while the real man is shunned by all but the executioner. On the other hand, it is not composed exclusively of evil characters - that would not be necessary. One of Shvarts's main points is that the same result can be obtained by a few confirmed villains playing on the weaknesses of others who have neither the will-power nor the inclination to oppose them, but who still have sufficient initiative to profit by the system as it stands.

In *The Shadow*, the society rests on the twin pillars of money and the bureaucratic system; the best representative of this combination is the Finance Minister, who is one of the few thoroughly bad characters in the play. Paralysed, and carried around by two lackeys, he is a grotesque figure who provides many of the visually comic (even farcical) moments of the play, but he is sinister as well as grotesque, and very dangerous. He is even prepared to threaten the opera singer Julia, whom he professes to love, with immediate downfall if she does not contribute her aid to the plot against the Scholar. It becomes obvious, however, from his conduct in the final scene, that his own interests rather than those of the State are uppermost in his mind. The fate of the Shadow is of no moment to him as long as his own future is secure.

It is this instinct for self-preservation which characterises most of the people who surround the throne. This is true not least of the two lesser villains, Annunziata's father, Pietro, and Cesare Borgia, the journalist, both retired ogres, and both of whom collaborate with the Shadow's plot and in return receive posts at court. Their gratitude, however, does not extend to showing loyalty in a crisis, and while the headless Shadow sits on the throne, they consider making a discreet withdrawal from the court. Saved from further embarrassment by the sudden return of the missing head, they thereafter manage to drift with the tide of events, first rejoicing at their ruler's recovery, then attempting to capture him at the order of the Princess and finally assisting the Scholar's departure with a courtesy which ill conceals their eagerness to see him gone. Presumably they, like several of Shvarts's lesser villains, are hoping that their master's downfall may provide even better opportunities for them.

Self-preservation is also a major motive in the behaviour of the singer Julia and the Doctor, both of whose characters show some redeeming features. As Akimov has suggested, in the same way as Borgia is a villain *manqué*, being too petty to qualify, so the Doctor would have liked to be a good man, but finds it too difficult a task in such a society and so has given up the struggle (65). He was originally a dedicated physician, but his idealism has been worn down by the bureaucracy. Now he deals mainly with the pampered patrons of the spa, gains a sense of achievement from various petty triumphs and finds that the best method of dealing with the world is to dissociate himself from it. His one attempt to help the Scholar (a piece of ancient lore, for use when dealing with recalcitrant shadows) is made almost against his will, and the information delivered furtively, with a plea for anonymity. In the final scene, however, he makes no attempt to hide his admiration for the Scholar: 'He acted like a madman, went straight ahead, didn't turn aside; he was executed - and now he's alive, more alive than any of you' (*s*, 307).

As for Julia, she, according to Annunziata, is the 'Girl who trod on the Loaf' from Andersen's tale (66).

65. N. Akimov, 'Skazka na nashei stsene', in his *O teatre*, L., 1962, 247-8.

66. 'The Girl who trod on the Loaf', *Andersen's Shorter Tales*, translated by Jean Hersholt, New York, 1948, 437-44.

For having thrown a loaf of bread into a puddle, to save
her new shoes from the dirt, she was swallowed up by the
mud, but, says Annunziata, 'She scrambled out again, and
since then she has been treading on everyone, on good
people, on her best friends, *even on herself* - and all to
save her new shoes, her new stockings and her new dresses
(*s*, 247)'. I have italicised what is perhaps the most
significant phrase, for Julia does have some finer feelings, but finds it expedient to trample on these in the
interests of self-preservation. She, like the Princess,
is attracted by the Scholar's honesty and simplicity and
even makes a tentative attempt to refuse the Minister's
request for her help in the intrigue against him, but it
meets with such a frightening reception that she speedily
capitulates. Finally, when he is restored to life, she
rejoices, although she says somewhat ruefully, 'Don't tell
me it's going to be fashionable to be good now? But that's
such hard work!' (*s*, 305). It is not impossible that the
contact with the Scholar has in some degree altered the
attitudes of Julia and the Doctor, but it is unlikely that,
even in their case, his influence would long outlast his
departure. Other pressures would be too great.

The Shadow, although written almost on the eve of
war, and while the rest of Europe was actually fighting,
is not aimed explicitly at Hitler and Nazism, as are its
precursor, *The Naked King*, and successor, *The Dragon*. By
1940, with Hitler not only well-established in power but
also the official ally of the Soviet Union, it was already
too late to write a comedy about a tyrannical incompetent
(the Shadow is nothing if not efficient), and as yet too
early to write a play about a dragon to be challenged and
fought to the death. What Shvarts could do, and did, was
censure a society which would allow itself to be dominated
by a Shadow.

The play contains many references to the traditional
features of capitalist Europe, which are dealt with in
Shvarts's own style. For example, owing to the unstable
situation, the country's businessmen are sending all their
gold abroad for safety (even their gold teeth), but business
is still booming, because foreign businessmen in similar
situations are doing the same, in the opposite direction.
Rich malingerers come to take the waters of the spa, in
conjunction with eight-course banquets, and even the
street-sellers peddle murderers' knives and fresh poisons.

There are also, as in *The Naked King*, other pieces of
satire with a more ambiguous application. The power of the
bureaucracy, which enables the Shadow to proclaim that 'It's
all here in this file: the Princess and you and he and the
present and the future' (*s*, 274), applies to the Soviet
situation as well. So does the Finance Minister's accus-

ation to Julia that her love-songs contain elements of political sedition. ('"Oh why am I not a meadow!" ... You're hinting that the farmers have too little land' (*S*, 273)). This kind of hypersensitivity was particularly appropriate to the Soviet context in view of the atmosphere of the late thirties, as also was Borgia's statement that 'The best time to get rid of someone is when he is sick or on holiday. Then he himself doesn't know who did it, and you can keep on excellent terms with him' (*S*, 257).

The Shadow is a play which relies to a considerable extent on its characters and their psychology, and external comedy of situation and language is less important than, for example, in *The Naked King* where the characters are less defined. There are a few instances of such comedy, however: the Finance Minister and his lackeys provide some moments of farce; the most obvious verbal conceit is the conversation between the two Ministers who understand each other literally 'from half a word', and converse for the most part in abbreviated grunts.

Predictably, some of Shvarts's traditional themes recur in *The Shadow*, notably, of course, the fight between good and evil. Here, however, the evil is much more concentrated than elsewhere, since the Shadow's *raison d'être* is to be a negative force. The important theme of work is also present in the Scholar's words: 'After all, it's us, the ones who work, who keep the world turning' (*S*, 290), but since his work seems to be more cerebral than practical, not much emphasis is attached to this aspect. The theme of the collective, which had characterised Shvarts's children's plays of the thirties, is naturally absent here, since except for Annunziata the Scholar is alone against the world.

The heroes of *The Naked King* were also isolated in a hostile environment, but they found support in the ranks of the townspeople, who played an important role in the final victory. In *The Shadow* there is nothing of that kind; all attention is concentrated on the court, and the common people appear only in one small scene leading up to the climax of the play. Here they are seen crowding for a glimpse of the new king through the palace windows and uttering suitably patriotic sentiments - when within earshot of the Captain of the Guard, Pietro. None the less Pietro is uneasy, for he sees a potential resistance to authority in the fact that people are living, being born and dying as usual while such important events are taking place in the palace. He even wonders what would happen if 'one day, just as calmly, just as stubbornly, all together, they ...' (*S*, 289). But there is no room for such an implied event in this play. The outcome is a moral victory, rather than a social revolution, and the Scholar and Annunziata depart, leaving the court basically unchanged, and unlikely to change. In fact, their departure (*Corporal*: The carriage is at the door. *Scholar*: Annunziata, let's go! (*S*, 309)) has, with justice, been compared to the famous finale of *Woe from Wit (Gore ot uma)*.

Compared with Shvarts's other main political fairy-tales, *The Naked King* and *The Dragon*, *The Shadow* is, perhaps because of the context of its writing, the least optimistic in atmosphere, having neither the frivolous gaiety of *The Naked King*, nor the strength of purpose which characterises *The Dragon*.

The première of *The Shadow* on 11 April 1940 was preceded by comparatively little advance publicity, as far as the journals were concerned. Although the play was, from the first, intended for the Comedy Theatre, there was no mention of it in the theatre's plans for the season as announced in July 1939. At this stage it was stated only that 'the theatre will be working on Soviet plays, the order of production of which has not yet been determined' (67). Several of these were listed, but the list did not include *The Shadow*. Nor was there any mention of the play at the end of the year, when the plans for the ten-day festival of Leningrad theatres in Moscow were announced (68). The Comedy Theatre subsequently put on three plays, including *The Shadow*, in Moscow in May 1940, but only the other two were mentioned at this early stage. Perhaps Akimov was becoming wary of announcing the advent of Shvarts's plays until their performance was a certainty.

Whatever the case, *The Shadow* was apparently mentioned for the first time in an article by Akimov in January 1940, in which he listed some of the plays for the remainder of the season, including *The Shadow* (69). He also published a brief contribution to the section devoted to plans for the future. In this section he mentioned that he was working on *The Shadow* and added that it was no easy task.

67. 'Leningradskie teatry v novom sezone', *Iskusstvo i zhizn'*, 1939, no. 7, 6.*

68. 'Dnevnik khudozhestvennoi zhizni', *Iskusstvo i zhizn'*, 1939, no. 11-12, 29.*

69. N. Akimov, 'O printsipakh igry', *Iskusstvo i zhizn'*, 1940, no. 1, 20.

'The play presents an enormous challenge in the field of
genuine theatricality and stagecraft, since this fairy-
tale abounds in the kind of theatrical effects to which
we have long been unaccustomed in our practical experience' (70). Not since the early thirties had there been
any demand for even the limited amount of 'magic' present
in *The Shadow* and in this heyday of socialist realism, the
very thought of a play set in fairyland required a considerable readjustment of attitudes.

The reaction to the first production of *The Shadow*
varied as to the degree of approval, but was generally
favourable (71). N. Zhdanov saw the satire as indirect, but
still sharp: 'True, this is not the kind of satire which
has a specific social target ... It is directed against
those vices which degrade human nature - unscrupulousness,
egoism, false pride' (72). An anonymous reviewer commended
the play for its novelty. 'It is no secret to anyone that
variety of genres is more a slogan than a reality in our
literature and particularly in drama. In this respect,
Shvarts's experiment deserves every possible commendation' (73). This point was also made by Akimov in an
article published in a booklet containing the play and
various comments about it in 1940. According to Akimov,
'Shvarts has chosen for his comedy a special genre, which
in these days is being developed by him alone - the
fantastic comedy-fairy-tale' (74). Other uniformly favourable reactions came from Ya. Grinval'd and A. Deich, both
writing apropos of the performances in Moscow during May
(75). I. Grinberg also considered the play worthy of
commendation, to the extent of writing two articles about
it within one month (76).

70. N. Akimov, 'Zamysly', *Iskusstvo i zhizn'*, 1940, no. 1, 48.*

71. I. L'vov, 'Skazka dlya vzroslykh', *Iskusstvo i zhizn'*, 1940,
no. 5, 30-2; N. Zhdanov, 'O poetike komicheskogo', *Teatr*, 1940,
no. 7, 95-101; 'Skazka dlya vzroslykh', *Literaturnyi sovremennik*,
1940, no. 5-6, 228-9.

72. N. Zhdanov, 'O poetike komicheskogo', 99.

73. 'Skazka dlya vzroslykh', *Literaturnyi sovremennik*, 1940,
no. 5-6, 229.

74. 'Skazka na nashei stsene', republished in *O teatre*, 245.

75. Ya. Grinval'd, *'Ten''*, *Vechernyaya Moskva*, undated May 1940,
since it also deals with the festival production , in TsGALI,
fond 2215, opis' 1, ed. khr. 327, list 1*. A. Deich, 'Dva spektaklya
Teatra komedii, *Moskovskii bol'shevik*, 26 May 1940.

76. I. Grinberg, 'Ten'. Prem'era v Teatre komedii', *Leningradskaya
pravda*, 17 April 1940, 3 and 'Uchenyi i ego ten'', *Literaturnaya
gazeta*, 10 May 1940.

Other critics, however, had reservations about the play. P. Markish saw a fault in what he considered to be 'excessive modernisation', which 'to a certain extent splits the fairy-tale style and causes a rent in the very fabric of the fantasy-pattern' (77). Mixed reactions also came from critics such as M. Yankovskii, V. Zalesskii and S. Zamanskii. Yankovskii's offering, written in February, before the première, mentioned Shvarts's first two plays for adults and then hailed *The Shadow* as the first real fairy-tale and definitive break with reality (he seemed to have forgotten about *The Naked King* by this stage). However, he added rather obscurely that 'Shvarts has not yet managed to find the necessary ending. The fairy-tale for adults still lacks the necessary completion' (78). What he had in mind was not disclosed. S. Zamanskii regarded *The Shadow* as one of the few contemporary plays in which the author's individuality made itself felt, but regretted that 'at the end of the play, the lampoon and the keenness of the characterisation have somewhat obscured the fairy-tale' (79). V. Zalesskii considered that the play was written 'seriously and with talent', but objected to the introduction of half-tones of evil (namely the Doctor and Borgia), which 'make it difficult to have a complete perception of the basic conflict, and make the play in Acts II and III seem somewhat contrived' (80).

The two least favourable opinions at that time came from M. Levidov and V. Shklovskii and are unusual for the period in that they both consist of very detailed appraisals of the play on literary, rather than political, grounds. Both critics considered that Shvarts had failed in an attempt to synthesise the techniques of Hoffmann and Andersen into one play, and regarded the attempt itself as futile because, as Levidov put it, 'Andersen thinks with his feelings, whereas Hoffmann feels with his thoughts' (81). Levidov, like Zamanskii and one or two others, considered that the 'lampoon' had been too strong for the 'fairy-tale', particularly in the last two acts. His main objection was to the 'realisation of metaphors', which, he said, was admissible in moderation as a 'purely

77. *'Ten''. Pravda*, 26 May 1940, 6.

78. 'Fantaziya i deistvitel'nost'', 14.

79. 'Zametki o dramaturgakh', unplaced, undated [May 1940], TsGALI, fond 2214, opis' 1, ed. khr. 327, list 16.*

80. *'Ten'*. Spektakl' Teatra Komedii', *Trud*, 26 May 1940.

81. 'Dramaturg i ego ten'', *Literaturnaya gazeta*, 10 June 1940, 5.

illustrative technique', but here had become 'the theme,
the main idea of the work'. This he regarded as the
fault of the author, because he had 'gone away from himself', and had written differently for adults than he had
for children (82). It would, however, surely be necessary
in some way to adapt one's style to a more adult audience.
Besides, the 'realisation of metaphors' in question - presumably the whole situation of the man and his shadow - is
a particularly effective one.

Shklovskii's analysis makes exactly the same points
and adds further detail (83). Among his minor objections
are that 'the King's court is straight out of an operetta',
that the play 'is continuously apologising for its own
lack of reality', and that the heroine, the 'girl of the
people' who is preferred to the Princess, is after all the
daughter of an ogre ('is that any better than the daughter
of a kulak-peasant?') The ending of the play disturbed
him, as being not sufficiently optimistic and definite:
'He ought not to leave the Princess ... that is capit-
ulation. The play becomes pointless'. He was also concerned about the Shadow, because he considered that its
relationship with its master was ill-defined and insufficiently motivated. '[The Shadow] has no character', he
claimed, not seeing that exactly this feature is the
essence of the Shadow, for it *is* nothing but the opposite
of the Scholar, and therefore needs no human motive.

In his summing-up, Shklovskii seemed to be judging
the play by the standards of the children's theatre, and
considered that 'although ... *The Shadow* is not a children's play, none the less it suffers from the failings of
all our fairy-tale plays', including a lack of what he called
'grand fairy-tale conflicts' (84). One might think that
the theme of a man fighting for his life against his own
shadow would qualify as a 'grand fairy-tale conflict', but
it apparently did not satisfy Shklovskii, and his final
comment is that 'the company of shadows is bad company for
a dramatist. This ironical world does not create great
art' (85). It is noteworthy that both these critics used
the children's theatre as a criterion in their judgement
of the play, since there was nothing even remotely similar
in the adult world.

82. Ibid.

83. 'O skazke', *Detskaya literatura*, 1940, no. 6.

84. Ibid, 4.

85. Ibid.

Although it is not stated, *The Shadow* presumably continued its run into a second season at the end of 1940, and was interrupted only by the outbreak of war, when the Comedy Theatre began a hasty search for material that was topical - Shvarts's and Zoshchenko's *Under the Lime Trees of Berlin (Pod lipami Berlina)*; suitable for air-raid conditions - an evening of short Labiche comedies; or on a historically patriotic theme - A. Gladkov's *The Foster-lings of Glory (Pitomtsy slavy)*. Under these circumstances, there was no place in the new repertoire for *The Shadow*, with its abstract satire against the capitalist world.

Nor did the play return after the war, since the post-war literary situation was no place for plays such as *The Shadow*. Besides, by 1949 the Comedy Theatre had problems of its own, culminating in the dismissal of Akimov from the directorship of the theatre. In fact, in an article in the August 1949 issue of *Teatr*, V. Zalesskii used the memory of *The Shadow* as ammunition in the campaign against the theatre, apparently forgetting his own, albeit qualified, approval in 1940. In his attacks on the theatre's 'one-sided' repertoire, Zalesskii singled out for criticism another of the play's 1940 commentators - N. Zhdanov, who had approved, among other things, the 'tech-nique of exposing the theatrical illusion' (86). Presum-ably there was also some kind of campaign afoot against Zhdanov as well, for his comments about *The Shadow* were now attacked as 'raptures over the spectacular for its own sake, a complete neglect of the realistic theatre, which he contemptuously terms "everyday" theatre' (87).

The play did not return to the stage until more than fifteen years after its original run. The first revival was at Moscow's Satire Theatre in 1958 under the direction of E. Garin and Kh. Lokshina, with music by Prokof'ev (première on 3 March), a production which ran on into the sixties. It is not surprising that this theatre should have taken up Shvarts's play since it had already re-established Mayakovskii on the stage earlier in the decade. Nor was it coincidence that the director was Shvarts's friend and former Comedy Theatre actor Garin. By 1960 the play was also enjoying a second run in the Comedy Theatre (première on 16 November) and a popularity even greater than before. This time the critics were united in welcom-ing the play's return, noting the extra emphasis given to

86. N. Zhdanov, 'O poetike komicheskogo', *Teatr*, 1940, no. 7, 99.

87. V. Zalesskii, 'Na lozhnom puti (Zametki o Leningradskom teatre komedii)', *Teatr*, 1949, no. 8, 41.

the satirical aspect in the new production, and, if they made any comment on this, regarding it rather as an improvement than otherwise (88).

This Leningrad production ran throughout the sixties, during which time the play was also performed by several other theatres. It was, for example, produced as an examination production in two of the Moscow theatrical colleges in the early sixties (the M.S. Shchepkin College in 1961 and the B.V. Shchukin College in 1962) and was also performed in the Moscow Youth Theatre *(Tyuz)* as a play for older children. This was a very lively and enthusiastic production which received a favourable review from Yu. Aikhenval'd, and was still running, at the rate of one performance each month, in 1975 (89). In 1971 a film was made which, like many films of plays, took considerable liberties with the text and the scenery, but still managed to retain a very Shvartsian atmosphere. The play has also been published several times, including a version in the journal *Literaturnyi sovremennik* which is particularly interesting as an example of Shvarts's tendency to become carried away by his imagination (90). This version (published before the première) includes dialogues, characters, even whole scenes, extremely funny and sometimes sharply satirical, but which would obviously have been a brake on the action, and were removed (presumably by Akimov) by the time the play was staged.

In addition to its successes within the Soviet Union, *The Shadow* has been produced in other socialist countries, particularly in East Germany (Berlin, 1947; Potsdam, 1956) and also in the West (for example, Zürich, 1948). Of these foreign productions, perhaps the most interesting is that which took place in Berlin in 1947. This one provoked a variety of reactions, due to the wide range of political opinion in post-war Berlin. The play was performed in Max Reinhardt's Deutsches Theater, under

---

88. For example: K. Kulikova, 'Dvadtsat' let spustya', *Leningradskaya pravda*, 25 November 1960, 3; Yu. Golovashenko, 'Chelovek i ten'', *Vechernii Leningrad*, 14 December 1960, 3; A. Viner, 'Ten'', *Teatr*, 1961, no. 3, 105-7; and V. Smirnova, 'Skazochnik na teatre', in her *Sovremennyi portret*, M., 1964, 261.

89. Yu. Aikhenval'd, 'Perekhodnyi vozrast', *Teatr*, 1970, no. 2, 51.

90. Publications include: a small booklet in 1940 *Ten' (K postanovke p'esy v Leningradskom Gosudarstvennom Teatre komedii)**; the journal *Literaturnyi sovremennik*, 1940, no. 3, 3-62; the small collection *Ten' i drugie p'esy*, L., 1956, and all three editions of the collected plays.

the direction of Gustav Grundgens, with the première on
3 April 1947.

Many of the Berlin newspapers, including some of
those under British, American and French licences,
approved of the play. Of those who had any reservations
about it, only one ('R.M.' in *Der Sozialdemokrat*, a
British-licensed paper) objected on political grounds to
the satire (91). Those of the Western critics who
approved (or at least did not disapprove) of the play,
in most cases failed to mention the political content, and
those who did tended to under-emphasise it.

One point which struck many of the critics was,
naturally, that *The Shadow* was extremely untypical as a
Soviet play. It was indeed a pleasant surprise for many
of the Western-oriented critics. Moreover, being German
and mindful of their national heritage, many of them made
comparisons with aspects of nineteenth-century German
literature, one even going so far as to distinguish elements of Rococo, Romanticism, Biedermeier and Second
Empire (92). Many mentioned the play's European origins,
some citing only Andersen, others Andersen and Chamisso,
while one critic appeared to be unaware of the influence
of the Dane, and concentrated on the alterations Shvarts
had made to 'our Peter Schlemihl' (93).

These various opinions provoked in their turn a
reaction from the Soviet side. The organ of the Soviet
military administration, *Sovetskoe slovo*, published an
article taking issue with some of the points raised by the
German commentators (94). The author noted that most papers
praised the play, but was reluctant to accept even praise
from those who had referred to the play as a simple fairy-
tale with no deeper meaning. He was also understandably
annoyed by the Germans' readiness to claim all the sources
and influences for *The Shadow*, even going so far as to
reject the 'pessimistic fatalist Hoffmann' (95). Instead,
he stood out for the 'revitalising truth of Andersen's

91. R.M., 'Lichtspiele um einen Schatten', *Der Sozialdemokrat*,
11 April 1947.

92. C. Ernst, 'Die Furchtsamkeit der Macht', *Der Kurier*, 5 April
1947.

93. L.M., 'Im Zauberreich der alten Märchen', *Spandauer Volksblatt*,
9 April 1947, 2.

94. M. Kunin, 'Realisticheskaya skazka', *Sovetskoe slovo*, Berlin,
5 May 1947.

95. Ibid.

fairy-tales, the soft, but irresistible irony of Chekhov
and the all-conquering Soviet humanism of Gor'kii' (96).
Unfortunately for the validity of his point, Hoffmann
is one of the two influences most widely agreed on (in
fact, implicit in the play from the second name of the
hero: Christian Theodor). Besides, *revitalising* truth'
is surely the last phrase which could be applied to this
particular Andersen story. However, the reference to
Chekhov, who was in fact Shvarts's favourite author, is
one which could with justice have been made much more
frequently. There is even a direct parallel in the play
itself, where the Doctor tells the Scholar about the
particular kind of fear aroused by the bureaucracy:

> I once knew a man of unusual courage. He would
> go bear-hunting with only a knife; once he went
> out after a lion with just his bare hands ... And
> this same man fell down in a faint when once he
> inadvertently jostled a privy councillor. (*s*, 283)

The echo of Chekhov's 'Death of a Clerk' (Smert'
chinovnika) is too loud to be ignored.

The last years of peace marked the beginning of a more
widespread interest in Shvarts's work. Observers of the
children's theatre had known of him since 1929 and in
general (at least after the heated argument provoked by
his first children's play) those who knew approved. However, at the end of the thirties, with *The Snow Queen*
(his first children's play to attain immediate currency
outside Leningrad) and *The Shadow* (his first play for
adults to reach the stage), he became known to a much
wider circle of theatre-goers than before, and made a
lasting impression. *The Shadow*, once seen (particularly
in a pre-war Soviet context), was not easily forgotten.
Unfortunately, however, the outbreak of the war and the
fate of his next few plays for adults undid much of the
good work begun by *The Shadow* in 1940, and it was many
years before he became generally known as a dramatist for
adults as well as for children.

It was after writing *The Shadow* and before the
German invasion in 1941 that Shvarts began what is perhaps
his best-known play as far as the West is concerned - *The
Dragon*. Chronologically, its writing spanned nearly the
whole period of the war, but the exact date of commencement is uncertain. There was a reference to a new Shvarts

96. Ibid.

play in July 1940, when the plans for the new season in
the Comedy Theatre included the statement that 'Evgenii
Shvarts will submit his new play to the theatre
shortly' (97). However, this is perhaps too early for it
to have been *The Dragon*. The following April a notice
appeared to the effect that the Board of Administration
for Artistic Affairs had commissioned plays from several
authors in connection with the twenty-fifth anniversary
of the Revolution, due in 1942 (98). Shvarts was among
those from whom a play had been ordered, and although the
commission was of necessity shelved with the advent of
war, it is not impossible that what he began to write at
that stage was Act I of *The Dragon*.

The invasion came on 22 June 1941, at which time the
Comedy Theatre was preparing for its summer tour to
Moscow, and Act I of *The Dragon* was being read. All plans
were, naturally, overset by the event; theatres and dramatists alike found themselves under an obligation to produce
topical material without delay. Shvarts, temporarily
abandoning *The Dragon*, rose to the occasion by producing,
within a very short time, the satirical revue (written in
conjunction with Zoshchenko) called *Under the Lime Trees of
Berlin*. This, however, was a short-lived production as the
worsening situation quickly rendered the optimistic tone
of the piece unrealistic. Then the blockade ring closed,
and Shvarts, after holding out for several months despite
ill-health, was finally almost forcibly evacuated to Kirov
in December 1941. He lived there for some time, still
writing plays, including one about the blockade and one or
two for children, but all the time he was still trying to
complete *The Dragon*. In the summer of 1943, Shvarts moved
to Dushanbe (then Stalinabad) to join the Comedy Theatre,
and one year later, in June 1944, he moved with them to
Moscow.

It is at this point that *The Dragon* becomes of
importance once again, and thus it will now be appropriate
to comment on the play itself. *The Dragon* is perhaps
Shvarts's best-known play as far as the Western world is
concerned, since it is apparently the one most frequently
translated (at least into English). The plot is based on
various traditional fairy-tale themes, but this is the
first major work in which Shvarts set out to create his own
fairy-tale, rather than to adapt a plot from another source.

97. 'Teatry v novom sezone', *Iskusstvo i zhizn'*, 1940, no. 7, 43.*

98. 'V Upravlenii po delam iskusstv pri Lengorispolkome',
Iskusstvo i zhizn', 1941, no. 4, 47.*

The hero of the play is Lancelot, a knight-errant who in his wanderings comes to a town which for the last four hundred years has been ruled by a tyrannical dragon. The creature exacts a crippling tribute from the townsfolk, and chooses for himself one of the most beautiful girls every year. He so dominates the town that people not only do not dare to speak out against him, but can even persuade themselves that they love him, and are quite unable to visualise life without him. In this atmosphere, Lancelot's sudden irruption into their peaceful existence and his declared intention to kill the Dragon are received without enthusiasm. Even the prospective sacrifice, Elsa, has so accustomed herself to the situation that she accepts her fate quite calmly, has no desire to be rescued, and in fact endeavours to persuade Lancelot to leave the town. This, however, is against his code of behaviour, and he challenges the Dragon to a fight. Help in this undertaking, in the form of arms and moral support, comes not from the townspeople but from five wandering master craftsmen, a Donkey and a Cat.

The fight duly takes place and the Dragon is killed, but Lancelot himself is sorely wounded and is taken away, near death, by the Cat and the Donkey. The townspeople rejoice for a time over the death of the Dragon, but quickly fall under the sway of the villainous Mayor. The latter, despite his feigned madness during the Dragon's regime, is sane enough to seize the opportunity provided by Lancelot's absence in order to proclaim himself the slayer of the Dragon, and to become a dictator no less tyrannical than the previous ruler. In this he is ably assisted by his son Heinrich, who, having been first Elsa's fiancé and later the Dragon's trusted servant, now adapts himself with equal ease to the position of his father's aide.

The Mayor is just about to follow the Dragon's example and force Elsa to marry him (once again assisted by Heinrich) when Lancelot, whom all had thought dead, returns from a long convalescence in a wood-cutter's hut. He imprisons the Mayor and his son and, together with Elsa, settles down to the task of obliterating all traces of the Dragon from the hearts and lives of the townsfolk.

The setting of *The Dragon*, as befits such a play written during the war years, is more reminiscent of the Grimms' fairy-tales than of Perrault's or Andersen's. This Germanic emphasis is visible in the names of the townspeople (Müller, Friedrichsen and so on) and in such details as the Gothic lettering on the Town Hall. However, *The Dragon* does not correspond to any one tale, but is a synthesis of some of the typical themes which reappear in numerous variations in the folk tales of many lands.

The motif of the tyrannical dragon is almost universal, as is that of the hero who kills him, thus saving the
heroine's life. It is also not uncommon in fairy-tales
for an impostor to take the place of the hero during the
latter's absence and try to marry the heroine. On these
bases the plot of this work is built. However, as in all
of Shvarts's plays, the original ideas have undergone
some adaptation. For example, the heroine is usually a
Princess, but here, as with the Swineherd in *The Naked
King*, the Soviet context suggested a more popular origin
and hence Elsa is the daughter of the town's archivist.

The theme of the impostor has also been readjusted.
Traditionally, only the heroine knows the truth and she
is sworn to secrecy on pain of death. In this play the
whole town is aware of the deception but will not say
anything because their spirit is broken. Elsa herself
will not subscribe to the lie, although she feels helpless
because she is sure that Lancelot is dead. However, her
refusal to marry the Mayor and her appeal to the townsfolk at the wedding are ignored.

Many of the small details of the play also stem from
fairy-tales. Talking animals, of course, are very common,
as are hats of invisibility, flying carpets and other
motifs which appear in this play. Other elements have
their origins in reality. Apart from the main political
parallel in the play, there are a host of other small
topical and satirical references which help to fill out the
basic story.

With regard to the play's political allegory, the
point of controversy has always been the identity of the
Dragon. On the surface, naturally, he was Hitler. His
origins are explicitly Germanic - he says that he first
appeared on a day when 'Attila himself had suffered a
defeat' (*D*, 322) and claims that 'the blood of dead Huns
flows in my veins' (*D*, 323). When described by Charlemagne,
the archivist, his aerial tactics in battle and use of
'poisonous smoke' (*D*, 317) are obviously reminiscent of the
methods of the German armed forces. The Dragon, like the
Shadow of 1940, but unlike the Naked King of 1934, is not
a comic figure. The lesson had been driven home by the
failure of *Under the Lime Trees of Berlin*; Hitler was not
funny, but dangerous.

However, a play about a tyrant - particularly a play
which uses allegory to make its points - can always
support as many different meanings as there are tyrants.
In this play, the Dragon has three heads which, when he
appears 'in mufti' (*D*, 320), manifest themselves as three
different people, and this feature lends itself to considerable variety of interpretation on stage. There is also a

convenient ambiguity in Charlemagne's words to Lancelot about the Dragon: 'while he is here no other dragon will dare to touch us ... I tell you, the only way to keep dragons away is to have one of your own' (*D*, 318-9). It is unlikely that Shvarts could have been unaware of the possibilities of equating the Dragon with Stalin, particularly since he had already established, in plays such as *The Naked King* and *The Shadow*, a pattern of introducing elements which could be equally well applied within or outside the Soviet Union. On the other hand, it would be a mistake to regard *The Dragon* as an exclusively anti-Soviet play. Shvarts's vision was broader than that.

The play's hero Lancelot is described as a 'professional hero' (*D*, 331). He is a synthesis of all the heroic elements in folklore, including Sir Lancelot and St George, and is also reminiscent of the Russian epic hero (*'bogatyr''*) tradition. He is, however, a very human and typically Shvartsian version of the conventional knight-errant. His enthusiastic 'A dragon? Great!' (*D*, 314) on hearing of the town's plight, and his practical, almost offhand, questioning of the Cat as to his opponent's size and equipment constitute an affectionately disrespectful view of the ancient traditions of chivalry. Later, in Act II, Lancelot gives Elsa a delightfully casual description of the hero's task: 'A dragon here, some ogres there, a few giants somewhere else. It keeps you busy' (*D*, 344). It is not always a particularly rewarding life, but Lancelot deals with all problems with the same cheerful confidence. He relates how he has been 'slightly wounded twelve times, seriously - five times, and fatally - three times' (*D*, 314)'... Thrice I have been fatally wounded, and by the very people I was trying, against their will, to save' (*D*, 319). In this case, too, he finds something of the same attitude amongst those he sets out to save.

Charlemagne and his daughter, when they first encounter Lancelot, are both quite resigned to Elsa's imminent fate and do not wish even to discuss it with Lancelot. Charlemagne even defends the Dragon against criticism, telling how the Dragon saved the town from cholera by boiling the lake with his breath, and has kept the townsfolk safe from gipsies (although it is only from him that they have learned to fear the gipsies). However, when the Dragon appears and announces his intention of dealing with Lancelot on the spot, rather than in fair fight, Charlemagne reminds him of the document he had signed long ago, relating to the rules of combat. This is the beginning of Charlemagne's support for Lancelot, and he justifies it somewhat apologetically to the Dragon: 'Here's a man who's trying to save my little girl. I mean, it's all right to love your child. That's allowed' (D, 325). From this point onwards he begins to hope for better things.

Elsa takes longer to emerge from her attitude of dumb resignation to the inevitable. She tries to object at the end of Act I when she is given a knife with which to kill Lancelot, but she takes the knife. Only in Act II, when she realises that she loves Lancelot and public- ly throws the knife down the well, does she begin to hope for life rather than wait for death.

The Mayor and his son Heinrich provide much of the comedy in the play, with their (quite justified) assump- tions that they should not trust each other in the least. In addition, the Mayor's various nervous disorders pro- duce some farcical scenes. The father-and-son team appears at times in the light of a pair of comic stage villains, a foil in the early stages to the more serious villainy of the Dragon. They are delighted to see their master die, for now their own chance has come. As the Mayor says of the townspeople, 'their late master has trained them so well that now they'll carry anyone who takes up the reins' (D, 358). Thus, Act III, with the town now under the heel of the Mayor, who is preparing to marry Elsa, is a conscious parallel to the situation in Act I, and many of the phrases used by the Dragon are now heard from the Mayor.

In *The Dragon* a particularly important role is played by the townspeople. In *The Naked King* and *The Shadow* the emphasis was on the ruler and his court rather than on the people. In *The Dragon*, however, the ruling class consists of only two or three people, so the towns- folk are proportionally more important. These people are basically good-hearted but after generations of subser- vience to the Dragon they have completely lost their independence. The people are very reluctant to help Lancelot, and reject Charlemagne for siding with him, or rather for being punished for so doing. As one of the citizens says: 'Personally, I have completely ceased to recognise you, ever since they put your house under guard' (D, 353).

When the fight begins, the townspeople do not immediately think of the prospect of freedom, but are resentful because their own petty concerns are being interfered with and their peaceful existence disrupted. In the course of the fight, however, as the Dragon is gradually discredited by defeat, the attitude towards Charlemagne changes to one of acceptance and friendship. Under the Mayor's regime the citizens revert to their original subservience and appear to accept the lie that he is the Dragon-killer. When reproached for this by Lancelot ('But you knew it wasn't he who killed the Dragon') one of them replies shamefacedly 'At home, I knew ... but on parade ...' (*D*, 382). This shows the same attitude as is found in *The Shadow*, where the people make loud patriotic statements for Pietro's benefit.

The Dragon is the only play for adults in which Shvarts made use of talking animals. Perhaps he used them here because Lancelot has so little support from people. The five craftsmen who give him magic aid are travellers, but in the Dragon's town only the animals will help. Elsa's Cat at first does not believe that Lancelot can beat the Dragon, but nevertheless advises him to try and is, in fact, the first living being to declare on his side. Lancelot also consults the town's dogs, who, he says, are the only 'real workers'. He sympathises with them because, as he says, 'You think it's easy to love people? After all, the dogs know perfectly well what kind of men their masters are. They cry over them, but they love them' (*D*, 334). Finally, he is helped by the stubborn Donkey, who carries him mortally wounded away from the fight and will not turn back, even when the Cat says he is dead. It is the Donkey who takes him to the wood-cutter's wife who cures him.

'Fairy-tale logic' is present in the play in instances such as the complaint of the maker of magic hats - that he has never been able to see how his creations suit the wearer, since both immediately become invisible when the hat is put on. One other instance is a reference to the contemporary situation, but could occur only in a fairy-tale context. As the fight begins, one of the citizens relates how he has just seen the sugar and the butter rushing out of the shops to hide from the sound of battle, and comments 'They're terribly nervous, those goods' (*D*, 353).

There are a great many references to the war in the course of the play. The first act, written in the tense period before the outbreak, has reflections of the contemporary atmosphere in the ever-present threat of the Dragon, his supposed geniality and the atmosphere of rather pessimistic fatalism prevailing in the town at the beginning of the play. As in *The Naked King*, there are direct references to various features of Nazism, such as the Dragon's persecution of gipsies, easily identifiable as Hitler's attitude to the Jews. There is also a reference to the unexpected invasion, when the Dragon says to Lancelot, 'I won't tell you when I'm going to start. Real war begins suddenly' (*D*, 347). The scene of the fight includes many cuts at war-time information and propaganda, in the shape of the various communiqués put out by the Mayor and Heinrich. By means of these they try to prove, against the evidence of the citizens' own eyes, that the Dragon is winning the fight, and that all his efforts to evade the invisible Lancelot, and even the loss of his heads, are well-planned military manoeuvres.

The ending of *The Dragon*, in keeping with the rest of the play, written once the enemy was out in the open, is much more positive than that of *The Shadow*. Lancelot returns to the town, deposes the Mayor and his son and reclaims Elsa. This time, in contrast with *The Shadow* and *The Adventures of Hohenstaufen*, there is no magical escape for the villains - they are most realistically imprisoned. Nor can any parallels be drawn between the heroes and heroines of *The Dragon* and *The Shadow*. The Mayor does suggest to Lancelot a similar ending to that of the earlier play: 'Take Elsa by the hand and leave us to go on living in our own way. That would be so humane, so democratic' (*D*, 382). Lancelot, however, is not prepared to desert the town. He sees a task ahead of him - to straighten out the lives of the townsfolk: 'We will have to kill the Dragon in each one of them' (*D*, 383). His final words are: 'And at last, after much hard work and many trials, we will be happy, very happy, in the end' (*D*, 384). As S. Babenysheva wrote, 'The happy ending for E. Shvarts is not only a victory over the enemy, it is a road leading into the future' (99).

According to Shvarts's diary, the play was finished on 21 November 1943. Shvarts then spent some time 'intending to write a new play' and 'then wrote a new version of *The Dragon*'. It is not clear to what extent this new version differed from the original, and when and why it was written (the diary entry is merely looking back over the work done during the past year) (100). D. Moldavskii has stated that, 'in its final form, the play was read by the author in the Central Committee of the Tadzhikistan Communist Party', and that, at that stage,

99.   'Obyknovennoe i neobyknovennoe chudo', *Novyi mir*, 1961, no. 2, 253.

100. Extract from Shvarts's diary, 15 December 1944, prepared for publication by K.N. Kirilenko as 'V dni ispytanii', in *Vstrechi s proshlym (sbornik neopublikovannykh materialov TsGALI SSSR)*, Book 1, M., 1972, 233.

no-one doubted that the Dragon was intended to represent Hitler (101). In any case the play, in some form or another, was being read aloud by the author in mid-January 1944, according to an unidentified Stalinabad newspaper. Meanwhile, according to the same report, Akimov had gone to Moscow to present it to the Committee for Artistic Affairs (102). Shvarts himself confirmed this and paid a special tribute to Akimov: 'Akimov is even more intelligent and sparkling than ever. It is thanks only to him that I finished writing *The Dragon* here. Now Akimov is in Moscow and I am waiting for news' (103). Later, Akimov mentioned that the play was passed by the Committee 'without a single correction' and 'approved and passed at all the preliminary viewings' (104).

The Dragon was also published at this time, in a collotype edition of five hundred copies. It was in this edition that the play was subjected to a vitriolic attack by Sergei Borodin (105). Borodin was appalled by the author's 'harmful, anti-historical, anti-social, vulgar attitude to contemporary reality' and his 'slander against the peoples who are languishing in the power of the Dragon'. He was amazed 'how hard a heart one must have, and how far away one must be from the common struggle against Hitlerism, to compose such a dragon-story'. To a considerable extent, the reason for these outbursts seems to lie in an insufficient understanding of the play's subtleties. He was, for example, shocked by the fact that, as he saw it, 'the inhabitants [of the town] are in raptures over their Dragon'. He then quoted several of Charlemagne's praises from Act I, and pointed out that this comes from a '*positive* character' (actually, however, some of the force of the play comes from the changing attitudes of Charlemagne). His next example was even less convincing. He quoted the Mayor's line: 'I'm so sincerely attached to our Dragon ... I'd even give my life for him' (*D*, 332), without making any value judgement on the Mayor's character or taking into account the fact that he is talking to Heinrich (the Dragon's lackey), and that the whole point of the scene is that he

101. 'Gospodin Drakon, Gerr Burgomistr i drugie', *Literatura i zhizn'*, 1 July 1962, 4.

102. 'Novaya p'esa E. Shvartsa *Drakon*', unplaced [Stalinabad paper], 18 January 1944, TsGALI, fond 2215, opis' 1, ed. khr. 322, list 51.*

103. Letter from E. Shvarts to L. Malyugin, 20 August 1944, in 'Iz perepiski Evgeniya Shvartsa', *Voprosy literatury*, 1977, no. 6, 226.

104. In *My znali Evgeniya Shvartsa*, 183.

105. S. Borodin, 'Vrednaya skazka', *Literatura i iskusstvo*, 25 March 1944, 3.

is being quite extravagantly sycophantic. Borodin then
went on to cast aspersions on Elsa, by the simple expedient of reciting a list of all the people she is prepared to marry in the course of the play - again, without
taking into account the conditions involved, or her
attitudes to the various situations. His conclusion was:

> The moral of this fairy-tale, its 'message',
> consists of the doctrine that there is no
> point in fighting dragons - they will only
> be replaced by other, smaller dragons - and
> anyway, the people are not worth breaking a
> sword for; while the knight fights only
> because he does not know how base are the
> people for whom he is fighting.(106)

This last claim is surely nullified by Lancelot's words:
'I love you all, my friends. Otherwise, why would I
have bothered with you ...' (*D*, 384).

This article is the only really serious attack on
The Dragon which I have found. Its author seems to have
been an enthusiastic, if unsubtle, patriot. In 1941 he
had written a historical novel about one of the famous
Russian heroic figures, Dmitrii Donskoi, and his victories
over the Mongols. It is interesting that his attack was
directed against the play solely in terms of its war-time
interpretation rather than as anything openly anti-Stalin.

However, the possibilities for other interpretations
were obvious to anyone who dared to admit them to himself.
L. Malyugin, prompted firstly by Borodin's attack and
secondly by the receipt of a copy of the play, wrote a
letter to Shvarts that is half-sympathetic and half-
congratulatory. He considered *The Dragon* to be one of
those plays, 'very rare in our times', which leave the
reader wishing they were longer (107). 'It is an angry
and sad work - there is about 8 times as much anger and
sadness in it as in your other plays. The people have got
so used to trouble, robbery, autocracy, injustice, that
nothing can surprise or upset them, even the news of their
own imminent death ... There is no longer any hope of
correcting the townspeople - they are poisoned by baseness
and lies. (Let us agree that this town is situated in
German territory - and that will be easier)' (108). The
strategic placing of the sentence in parentheses leaves

---

106. Ibid.

107. Letter from L. Malyugin to E. Shvarts, 8 April 1944, in 'Iz
perepiski Evgeniya Shvartsa', *Voprosy literatury*, 1977, no. 6, 228.

108. Ibid.

one in no doubt of Malyugin's interpretation.

Meanwhile, back in Stalinabad, Shvarts's diary
for 28 March 1944 noted that 'rehearsals for *The Dragon*
are going ahead at full speed. Akimov went down with
'flu three days ago, which is slowing up the work.
It looks as though *The Dragon* is turning out well' (109).
In June, the Comedy Theatre arrived in Moscow, with a
repertoire which included *The Dragon*. On the afternoon
of 4 August the one and only performance took place,
which Akimov referred to as the 'première', but which
Tsimbal, more credibly, calls a 'public viewing' (110).
A première would surely have appeared in the entertainment guide in *Pravda*, and it would not have taken place
in the afternoon. The date for this performance,
although apparently nowhere mentioned in published
accounts, was obtained from sources in the Comedy Theatre.
In any case, if I. Shtok was correct in his statement
that the play was performed in the Operetta Theatre,
the event must have taken place between 10 June (when the
theatre arrived in Moscow) and 8 August, when it moved
from the Operetta Theatre to another venue (111). It
must have been an afternoon performance, since a normal
evening performance of another play was scheduled for that
day in *Pravda*.

Many years later, Akimov described how, in the
course of this performance, he was summoned to a 'very
disturbed Committee chairman' and told not to repeat the
play. He commented:

> No reason was given, indeed none could have
> been given; much later it emerged that some
> over-vigilant official of that time had seen
> in the play something which was not there at
> all.(112)

This is the only available suggestion that the play was
banned for any more specific reason than the general
'slander against the people' seen by Borodin. Of course,

109. Extract from Shvarts's diary, 28 March 1944, in E. Shvarts,
'V dni ispytanii', 232.

110. Akimov in *My znali Evgeniya Shvartsa*, 183; Tsimbal's introduction to Shvarts, 'Fantaziya i real'nost' (iz arkhiva Evgeriya
Shvartsa)', *Voprosy literatury*, 1967, no. 9, 176.

111. *Rasskazy o dramaturgakh*, M., 1967, 142.

112. In *My znali Evgeniya Shvartsa*, 183.

Akimov's words could also refer to such a view, but considering the subsequent return to relative favour of the play by the time Akimov was writing, it is likely that he would have dealt faithfully with any such general objection. Besides, such a reason 'could have been given'. I. Shtok, who was in Moscow at the time and acquainted with Shvarts, later wrote of *The Dragon* as a 'colourful anti-fascist play' (113). With reference to the ban, his version was that 'somebody decided that this fairy-tale was not on the same level as the monumental struggle of the people against Hitler's hordes, and that it insulted the feelings of sacred hatred. The play was taken off. And quite unjustifiably' (114). This version coincides with Borodin's attitude to the play, but is perhaps insufficient to explain its removal, particularly in view of the approval accorded to the play elsewhere, precisely on this anti-Nazi level.

It is ironic that on the same day, 4 August 1944, an article by M. Zagorskii appeared, reproaching the Comedy Theatre for bringing such an unsatisfactory repertoire, and commenting 'in these years of the great war, a theatre has no right to talk to the audience about trifles, and not to give its response to the events which have shaken the whole country' (115). Meanwhile, the one play which would have answered such a demand was being quietly removed from the stage.

At the end of November 1944 there was a discussion of the play in the Committee for Artistic Affairs (116). The fact that this discussion was referred to by Tsimbal as being 'in connection with the staging of the play' indicates that the August prohibition was not regarded as final. Moreover, Shvarts recorded a fortnight after the discussion: 'Today I went with Akimov to the Repertoire Committee to talk about a new version of *The Dragon*' (117). Neither author nor director, apparently, was prepared to let the play go without a fight.

At the November meeting some very complimentary comments were made by such people as the playwright N. Pogodin, the puppet theatre director S. Obraztsov and the

113. 'Evgenii Shvarts', in his *Rasskazy o dramaturgakh*, 142.

114. Ibid, 143.

115. 'Spektakli Teatra komedii', *Vechernyaya Moskva*, 4 August 1944, 3.

116. *Evgenii Shvarts*, footnote, 197.

117. Extract from Shvarts's diary, 15 December 1944, in E. Shvarts, 'V dni ispytanii', 233.

writer I. Erenburg. The latter is said to have emphasised that the play was devoted to the 'moral rout of
fascism', according to Tsimbal's account of the meeting (118). Tsimbal declared that 'the greatest attention was attracted by the political sub-text of the tale,
to be more precise, those direct political associations
which it calls to mind' (119). The last half-sentence is
a masterpiece of non-clarification, but despite the
cautious wording, the 'associations' referred to were
those connected with the war, at least according to the
reactions quoted by Tsimbal. Shvarts is reported to have
said at some stage of the discussion: 'One must not
write works which are simply interesting or entertaining;
one must write works which are desperately needed', and
later, when someone suggested he remove the whole incident
of the second government and the Mayor's wedding, his
reply was that 'the idea of removing everything political
from the tale does not interest me' (120). The Mayor's
takeover has always been seen as a reference to the
Allies, and perhaps it was felt that it would not be
altogether tactful to include it. However, in its more
general context, the incident merely points out that the
removal of one tyrant does not preclude the arrival of
another if the people are still mentally subservient
enough to accept it.

One interesting sidelight on the situation can be
found in the Central State Archive of Literature and Art
(TsGALI), and concerns the much-quoted lines of Charlemagne used by anyone who wants to prove that Shvarts meant
the Dragon to be Stalin: 'While he is here, no other
dragon will dare to touch us ... the only way to keep dragons away is to have one of your own' (*D*, 318-19). In
the archive there is a typed copy of the play with
author's and director's annotations, dated (on the file,
at least) 1943 - presumably the copy Akimov worked from
in his production. The director's corrections are in
coloured pencil and Shvarts's in purple ink. In this
copy, that particular section is *enclosed in brackets* in
purple ink (121). This, of course, proves nothing except
that, after he had written the play, Shvarts looked a
second time at those lines.

118. *Evgenii Shvarts*, 197.

119. Ibid.

120. Quoted by V. Golovchiner in 'Put' k skazke E. Shvartsa', 183,
citing TsGALI, fond 2215, opis' 7, ed. khr. 21, list 8.

121. TsGALI, fond 2215, opis' 1, ed. khr. 17, list 6.

Sixteen years passed. Whatever effort may have been expended in the way of new variants and visits to committees produced no results. The play was officially 'dead', but unofficially by no means gone. It was, in fact, being read, in hand-written or typewritten copies by various interested people throughout the remainder of the forties and the fifties. No attempt was made to stage it again, of course, since the latter half of the forties was a bad time to try to revive anything in the least degree controversial. Besides, in 1949 Akimov was dismissed from the Comedy Theatre and returned only in 1956. And even then, it was not until six years (and three more Shvarts productions) later that he returned to *The Dragon*.

Meanwhile, the play and its 1944 production were occasionally mentioned in various contexts during the late fifties and the sixties. D. Moldavskii, in a review of the 1956 selection *The Shadow and other plays (Ten' i drugie p'esy)*, noted that the book was not a full collection of Shvarts's plays, since it lacked his children's plays of the thirties and also his 'philosophical comdey *The Dragon* which N.P. Akimov has worked on', and expressed the hope that such plays would soon be published and produced once more (122). (Moldavskii, one of the younger generation of critics at that time, had not only been present at the reading of Act I of *The Dragon* in Leningrad in 1941, but had spent much of the war in Stalinabad.) *The Dragon* was mentioned again in the programme for the Comedy Theatre's production of Shvarts's *The Tale of a Young Couple (Povest' o molodykh suprugakh)* (123). Another reference is in Akimov's afterword to the 1958 edition of the same play (124).

The Dragon was published in the original 1960 collection of Shvarts's plays. Also in 1960, in a history of Soviet theatre, I. Shneiderman had written a chapter on Leningrad theatres during the war, which mentioned the play in some detail and with considerable approbation, but with no reference to its untimely removal (125). Since the chapter was on 'Leningrad theatres' rather than 'Leningrad playwrights', the author was under no obligation to mention the play at

122. 'Puteshestvie v skazochnyi mir', *Leningradskaya pravda*, 16 September 1956.

123. TsGALI, fond 2215, opis' 1, ed. khr. 308, list 4.

124. Akimcv, in Shvarts, *Povest' o molodykh suprugakh*, M., 1958, 97.

125. I. Shneiderman, 'Leningradskie teatry' in N.G. Zograf and others, eds., *Ocherki istorii russkogo sovetskogo dramaticheskogo teatra*, II,1935-1945, M., 1960, 681.

all. Therefore, he must have regarded it as being of sufficient value and interest to overcome the disqualification of its non-run (not to mention the obvious embarrassment of its sudden disappearance) and still deserve a mention. Later there appeared a small documentary history of the Comedy Theatre, comprising pictures and biographies of the troupe, scenes from productions and lists of all productions between 1929 and 1963 (126). This, besides mentioning the 1962 production, not only includes one photograph from the 1944 version, but also lists the play as the only new production for 1944 (127). Perhaps its inclusion is partly due to the fact that without *The Dragon* there would have been no new plays listed for that year.

By contrast, M. Yankovskii's book on the Comedy Theatre, written five years later in 1968, evaded the question completely by avoiding all mention of the play. This would be a legitimate, if somewhat pedantic, approach, since it had no noticeable run on the stage in 1944. However, Yankovskii also managed to avoid mentioning the revival in the sixties, either amongst the 'productions of earlier plays', where he included the 1960 version of *The Shadow*, or, failing that, amongst the 'new comedies by Soviet authors, first produced in this theatre' (128). Since he could not possibly have been unaware of the play's existence, the omission can either be explained by a (perhaps oversensitive) response from Yankovskii to the play's decreased acceptability after those five years, or by straight censorship. The coincidence of Yankovskii's book being 'passed for printing', with no reference to *The Dragon* on 23 August – three days after the invasion of Czechoslovakia – gives scope for much speculation, but may be fortuitous.

Meanwhile, back in the theatre – in 1962, at the height of Khrushchev's de-Stalinisation campaign – Akimov, now more firmly established than ever before at the head of the Comedy Theatre and doubtless encouraged by the success of the new production of *The Shadow*, returned to his protégé *The Dragon*. The première was on 29 May 1962, towards the end of the 1961-62 season. In the three-and-a-half weeks before the end of the season (21 June), the play was shown eight times (129).

126. M.A. Shuvalov, ed., *Teatr komedii (al'bom)*, L., 1964.

127. Ibid, 31.

128. Yankovskii, *Leningradskii Teatr komedii*, 138, 154.

129. 29 and 30 May; 5, 6, 11, 12, 18 and 19 June; the double dates are probably due to technical considerations, since the play requires a lot of special effects.

The reception of the 1962 production on the part of the critics was surprisingly lukewarm, not to say silent. Papers such as *Literaturnaya gazeta* and even theatrical periodicals such as *Teatr* and the fortnightly *Teatral'naya zhizn'* (admittedly, all Moscow-based) seem to have ignored the play altogether, except for a brief note to the effect that the première had taken place (130). Even that was three months overdue, since it occurred in the section of news from all over the Soviet Union, and the turn of the Leningrad region did not come around until August. It could well be that everyone was waiting for a lead, no-one wishing to be first to praise or condemn, in case they were later 'proved wrong'. The only review of the play I could find was the one by D. Moldavskii and the greater part was devoted to comments on the history and signifi- cance of the play, rather than to a review of the current production (131). Moldavskii mentioned the writing of the play in Tadzhikistan and referred to the 'first version of the production' which was also prepared there, although giving no details of its fate. Subsequently, he devoted considerable space to the message contained in the play.

> Years have passed since that time. Many things have gone out of date and passed away, but Shvarts's fairy-tale still lives – a wise and humanistic tale, full of hatred for blind militarism, oppression, deceit and lies. *The Dragon* is an anti-fascist and anti-militaristic play. The point of the work has not passed away ... We, who saw or read this play during the war years, could very clearly feel in which direction it was aimed; the blow was directed at those in the West who love to make others do their dirty work for them ...

> But the play was not only a response to the events of those years. *The Dragon* – and this is emphasised in the new version of Akimov's production – exposed the morals of a society which lives by the principle of 'dog eat dog' ...

> In Shvarts's hands, the ancient tale attacks not only the dumb and malicious forces of war, but also hypocrisy, sanctimoniousness and cowardice. This is emphasised by the director ...

130. *Teatral'naya zhizn'*, 1962, no. 16, 15.*

131. 'Gospodin Drakon, Gerr Burgomistr i drugie', *Literatura i zhizn'*, 1 July 1962, 4.

In the new production of the Leningrad Comedy
Theatre, we once again encounter Evgenii Shvarts
and his satire - humane, noble and inexorable,
unmasking the real character of our enemies,
however they may disguise themselves with masks
and fine words.(132)

Despite his references to more general associations,
the critic's words in the early part of the article seem
to place him in the school of thought that emphasised the
1962 parallels with West Germany. This is borne out by
the same writer's words in an article five years later,
referring to the posthumous success of *The Naked King*
and *The Dragon*.

In these plays people looked for, and found,
elements of the kind of criticism which was
able to arise only after the XX Communist Party
Congress. I think that Evgenii L'vovich
himself would have been most surprised by the
parallels which suddenly arose in the minds of
the audience.(133)

Another of the few contemporary comments did not
actually mention *The Dragon* by name. D. Zolotnitskii,
writing in rather faint praise of Akimov and his theatre,
commented:

The workshop of dramatists belonging to the
Comedy Theatre began during the lifetime of
Evg. Shvarts, the author who was closest to
Akimov. Now they should, if not actually
replace Shvarts, then set out upon a wide
search in the field of contemporary repertoire.(134)

This was written at the beginning of the 1962-63 season
and, bearing in mind the fact that *The Shadow* had been
running for two years already, while *The Dragon* had dominated the end of the previous season with eight performances in one month, the implication seems to be that,
with all due respect to Shvarts, it was time for a change
in the repertoire. This wish was, in part, to be ful-
filled.

The 1962-63 season opened on 1 September 1962. *The
Dragon* did not return to the stage until 1 November, but
in the next three weeks there were five performances.

132. Ibid.

133. D. Moldavskii, 'Poeticheskii i skazochnyi mir Evgeniya
Shvartsa', *Nash Sovremennik*, 1967, no. 3, 109.

134. 'Zaboty komedii', *Neva*, 1962, no. 9, 196.

On 1 December Khrushchev made his famous outburst at the art exhibition at the Manezh, which signalled the start of a new campaign. However, as Priscilla Johnson observed:

> In the early days after the visit to the Manezh, the reaction confined itself mainly to sculpture and painting. Apart from the general dynamic of Soviet society, there was no sign to show that it would spread to other art forms as well. (135)

Certainly there was no visible effect on *The Dragon*, which continued its run with four performances in December and another four in January. By February 1963, however, the campaign had spread to literature. There were only two performances of *The Dragon* in February, and there were another two in the first days of March, before the campaign reached its peak with the meeting of writers and Party leaders in the Kremlin on 7 March. This meeting, with speeches by Khrushchev and Party Secretary Il'ichev designed to halt the de-Stalinisation process, was followed by similar meetings in provincial centres, of which the most important was held in Leningrad on 14 March. Leningrad was living up to its tradition, and many at the meeting were insufficiently repentant of their mistakes, including Akimov. According to Priscilla Johnson, 'signs of dissent were censored out of accounts of the meeting in *Pravda*, March 15, *Sovietskaya kultura* and *Literaturnaya gazeta*, March 16. A report in *Leningradskaya Pravda* was, however, more revealing' (136). This latter report was quoted extensively in the *New York Times*. On the subject of Akimov, the Leningrad paper apparently asserted that his speech,

> devoted to problems of satire, did not satisfy members of the audience. It showed little sincerity. It was impossible to understand what position the speaker was supporting, what his attitude towards the questions under discussion was. Comrade Akimov avoided answer to [Leningrad Party Secretary Tolstikov's] just criticism of some of his productions. (137)

Among these productions was *The Dragon*, which was attacked for being ideologically 'ambiguous'. The *New York Times* commented:

135. *Khrushchev and the Arts. The Politics of Soviet Culture 1962-64*, Cambridge, Mass., 1965, 10.

136. Ibid., 29, footnote 97.

137. Anonymous report, quoted by Theodore Shabad, 'Modernists defy Leningrad Reds', *New York Times*, 20 March 1963, 5.

Some viewers have accepted the [play's] allegory
as applying to West Germany today, but others
see it as a call to combat the remnants of
Stalinism. Hence Mr Tolstikov's concern about
the play's 'ambiguous ideological message'.(138)

Despite Tolstikov's attacks, however, the honours
in this part of the encounter went to Akimov, who published a statement on 14 March - the day of the meeting,
thereby ensuring for himself the last word (139). The
statement combined an enthusiastic attitude to Soviet
art with what seemed like suitable respect for the outcome of the 7 March meeting. However, since the author
of the piece was Akimov, whose every word needs careful
scrutiny, the final effect was a powerful apologia for
such plays as *The Dragon*:

At the meeting between party and government
leaders and the representatives of the artistic
intelligentsia, a great number of very important
questions were posed and resolved, concerning
the development of our Soviet art ...

We need works of a healthy, optimistic art, an
incitement to production, in all the creative
forms and genres of socialist realism. We
need to produce works of a high standard of
artistry and ideas [*ideinost'*] in order to
satisfy the demands of the people.

And these will be produced! (140)

The emphasis on '*all* the creative forms and genres'
indicates that Akimov had *The Dragon* in mind, and the
conspicuous absence of half the usual 'Party and people'
cliché shows just how little respect he had for Party
campaigns. The use of the word *ideinost'* is also typical Akimov. From most other Soviet pens it would be
translatable as '[orthodox] ideological content', and
certainly would be read as such by those he was seeking
to delude, but in Akimov's vocabulary it undoubtedly
reverts to the more basic, literal meaning.

However, this small triumph proved to be a Pyrrhic
victory. Obviously, firm measures were subsequently
taken by the authorities, for after the Moscow and
Leningrad meetings in March 1963, *The Dragon* was

138. Ibid.

139. N. Akimov, 'Uverennost'', *Literaturnaya gazeta*, 14 March 1963,
3.

140. Ibid.

performed only thrice more - once on 19 March, again on 1 April and finally, near the end of the season, on 18 May. Given that Akimov was a man not to be influenced by mere atmosphere, it is probable that an effort was made to remove the play in mid-season, and that considerable persistence was required in order to stage those last three performances. *The Dragon* did not reappear in the following season.

Like *The Naked King*, *The Dragon* also underwent certain changes in the course of its run. In this case, however, the cuts were fewer; partly because the run was shorter, and partly because the play was so full of embarrassing parallels and references that the censors - already hampered by the fear of making allusions more obvious by cutting them - would not have known where to start. As a result, Charlemagne's speech about the advantages of having one's own dragon (*D*, 319) appears to have remained, and also, possibly, the Mayor's speech about the townsfolk after the Dragon's death ('Their late master has trained them so well that now they'll carry anyone who takes up the reins' (*D*, 358)). On the other hand, the reference during the fight to the disappearance of sugar and butter from the shops suddenly became embarrassingly topical in a Soviet context, and was removed after 1 June 1962, when Soviet butter prices were raised (141).

Since 1962, attempts to revive *The Dragon* have been few and far between. Many people know of (though few remember much about) a student production at Moscow University 'in the early sixties' (according to the general consensus) which is also said not to have lasted more than a few performances (but this, of course, is normal for student plays). I myself observed the failure of yet another attempt, by a group of students from various tertiary institutions in Moscow in 1975. After several months of rehearsals, the headmistress who had agreed to allow the performances to be held in her school read the play for the first time - and withdrew her permission. It is also claimed that there was a plan for a new production of the play in 1968 (theatre unspecified), which was never realised owing to the sudden tightening of Party control following the Czechoslovakian events in August of that year (142).

Meanwhile, since 1962 it seems that *The Dragon* is never mentioned by critics without approbation. Those

141. Information from the same personal source as in the case of *The Naked King*.

142. Corten, 'Evgenij Švarc', 40.

wishing to list the best of Shvarts's plays in a
'general' article almost invariably include this one.
Yu. Borev compared Shvarts (and particularly *The Dragon*)
to Brecht, and extolled him as an exponent of the
'intellectual drama in socialist realism' (and, surely,
to join the ranks of the 'socialist realists' must be
regarded as the ultimate in respectability) (143). A.
Lebedev in 1968 was equally approving of the play (144).
He deplored the early lack of attention to Shvarts's
works, while his comment on the 'theoretical misunder-
standing which for so long burdened ... the destiny' of
Shvarts's dramatic legacy and his claim that 'we saw *The
Dragon* just at the moment when at last we were fully able to
understand it' indicate that he had at least as good a sense
of the 'irony of history' as he said Shvarts had (145).

In the meantime, whatever the irregularities of
The Dragon's progress within the Soviet Union, abroad -
both in the West and in East European countries - it has
been doing well ever since the beginning of the sixties.
The first Polish production, at the Teatr Ludowy in Nowa
Huta, was in June of 1961, nearly a year before the
Comedy Theatre revival (146). Since 1962 it has been
produced on the stage in Czechoslovakia, USA (Phoenix
Theatre, New York, 1963), France (Théâtre des Nations,
Paris), Italy (Teatro 'Struttura', Messina, 1973), Britain
(Royal Court Theatre, London) and perhaps most notably in
the GDR, where it ran at the Deutsches Theater in Berlin
from 1965 at least until 1975. I have been informed by
someone who saw this Berlin production towards the end of
the sixties that members of the theatre told him that it,
too, had been removed from the stage at the beginning of
its run and only brought back after considerable argument
and adaptation, and with the addition of a programme note
which applied the allegory firmly to the capitalist West.
There has also been an opera called *Lanzelot* in the GDR
(music by Paul Dessau).

In fact, the play is probably more widely known outside the Soviet Union than inside. If the name Shvarts
means nothing to a Westerner, the mention of *The Dragon*

143. 'Sotsialisticheskii realizm i drama-kontseptsiya', in
Sotsialisticheskii realizm i khudozhestvennoe razvitie chelovechestva,
M., 1966, 411.

144. 'Skazka est' skazka', *Teatr*, 1968, no. 4.

145. Ibid, 38.

146. Poster, TsGALI, fond 2215, opis' 1, ed. khr. 312, list 1. The
play was translated by Jerzy Pomianowski, presumably either from one
of the very rare copies of the 1960 edition or from a *samizdat* copy.

may. But inside Russia, although it may be possible to
jog the memory of a Muscovite with a mention of *The Naked
King*, or that of a Leningrader with *The Shadow*, if they
do not already know Shvarts's work, they will never have
heard of *The Dragon*. On the other hand, amongst those
Russians who do know his plays, knowledge is usually
accompanied by a considerable enthusiasm and respect for
him as a playwright, and in many cases by a conviction
that *The Dragon* is his best play.

The years after the war were very lean times for
Soviet literature in general, and for a writer such as
Shvarts they meant an almost complete retreat into silence.
Except for two children's films and some minor works in
other genres, none of Shvarts's work during the last
years of Stalinism managed to pass through the fine net of
the Zhdanov period and the 'no-conflict theory'. This,
however, does not mean that he was not still writing, and
some of the works which appeared many years later had their
origins in this apparently fruitless period.

For example, a play which appeared only three weeks
before Shvarts's death, *The Tale of a Young Couple*, was in
fact of the same vintage as *The Dragon*. This is the only
play for adults since *The Adventures of Hohenstaufen* to
combine reality with fantasy, but even this is a basically
realistic work, and the fantasy is very much confined to
the outer frame. The play is a study of the first year in
the married life of a young couple named Marusya and
Serezha. The action follows their relationships with their
friends and with each other, through occasional jealousies,
minor quarrels and reconciliations. Finally, after one
particularly violent and unreconciled dispute, Serezha has
to leave on business, without seeing Marusya to say good-
bye. While he is away Marusya falls ill and nearly dies,
which, not surprisingly, brings about a complete reconciliation on all points, and the play ends as Serezha is
about to leave on another business trip, but this time
taking Marusya with him. The occasional sentimentality
and melodrama of the work detract somewhat from its
value, but the presentation of the couple and their
friends has plenty of life and movement.

The fantastic element is represented by two life-
size toys - a doll and a teddy bear, given to Marusya as
wedding presents. They are very old and have seem many
families in their time, so they are also very wise, and
provide a kind of Greek-chorus commentary on the action.
Since, however, as emphasised by the Doll in the very
first line, 'Dolls can't talk' (*TYC*, 511), they are isolated from Marusya and Serezha. The young people fre-

quently talk to them when alone, and they give their owners much good though unheeded advice on occasion, but the only times when a two-way conversation takes place are once when Marusya is ill and feverish, and once when Serezha is half-asleep.

Thus, once again Shvarts is creating deliberate ambiguity as to whether the play is a fairy-tale or a realistic play. Akimov, despite the fact that he is said to have played down the role of the toys in his production, was in no doubt that 'none the less, [the] play is a fairy-tale' (147). At any rate it displays an attitude commonly to be found in Shvarts's fairy-tale plays - that the traditional 'happy ending' is, in fact, only a beginning, or at least the next step to a continuation. This play begins where most fairy-tales leave off, and shows that 'living happily ever after' is less of a sinecure than is usually implied.

The Tale of a Young Couple was written in 1944 when Shvarts was in Stalinabad with the Comedy Theatre. At that stage, the play was called *One Year (Odin god)*. However, according to Akimov, 'for some reason it aroused doubts in the Chief Repertoire Committee' and was rejected (148). Five years later, in 1949, Akimov returned to the subject of *One Year*, and this time he managed to have it accepted by the authorities. That summer Shvarts was with the Comedy Theatre on its tour to Sochi, and was reworking the play for them. Akimov's wife, the Comedy Theatre actress E. Yunger, recalled how Shvarts, being a very gregarious man, had to be locked into his hotel room to encourage him to write, instead of talking to the rest of the troupe (149). The resourceful Shvarts, however, made good use of the balcony, and was discovered holding forth to an admiring crowd of actors collected in the street below. Unfortunately, in August 1949 an increasingly vicious campaign against the Comedy Theatre culminated in the dismissal of Akimov, and the project to stage *One Year* lapsed.

Akimov, however, was a very persistent man; once restored to his Comedy Theatre after Stalin's death, and having made a success of another Shvarts fairy-tale,

147. N. Akimov's afterword to the first edition of Shvarts, *Povest' o molodykh suprugakh*, M., 1958, 99.

148. In *My znali Evgeniya Shvartsa*, 184.

149. Ibid., 228-9.

The Ordinary Miracle (Obyknovennoe chudo), he returned
yet again to the unstaged *One Year*. The journal *Teatr*
noted that 'in October E. Shvarts's comedy *The Tale of a
Young Couple* will be staged' (150). The change of name
is typical of Shvarts's plays, but while most of his
plays had one name at a time, this one was referred to
severally as *The Tale of a Young Couple*, *The First Year
(Pervyi god)*, and *Two Together (Vdvoem)*, all within this
month of October (151). The estimated time of appearance
in the *Teatr* statement proved to be extremely optimistic
(unless the following October was meant), for the première did not take place until 30 December 1957.

This delay was presumably connected with the slow-
ing-down of the literary and political Thaw, brought on
by the lesson of the Hungarian uprising and other factors.
During 1957 various works and authors, approved of (at
least silently) in 1956, fell into disfavour. A discussion on Dudintsev's novel *Not by Bread Alone (Ne
khlebom edinym)*, scheduled to take place in the Leningrad
Writers' Union, was cancelled without notice or explanation, and Shvarts was among the first to sign a telegram
of protest. As he confided later to V. Ketlinskaya: 'I
don't like the novel much, but there ought to be an open
discussion, without administrative interference' (152).
Throughout the year, the situation deteriorated steadily,
so that the only surprise occasioned by the late appearance of *The Tale of a Young Couple* is that the play
appeared in what was perhaps the most inclement period of
the Khrushchev decade. If the delay was attributable to
administrative factors, then its ultimate appearance can
only be regarded as a tribute to Akimov's persistence.

The play when it did appear 'aroused great interest
and sparked off a controversy' (153). Unlike some of its
contemporaries, it does nothing to show up the faults in
various Soviet types and their attitudes, but it is none
the less typical of one aspect of Thaw literature (despite
the fact that it was written about ten years before the
Thaw began) in that it concentrates on individuals and
their personal relationships. In May 1958, Akimov
defended the play against accusations of preoccupation

150.   'V novom sezone', *Teatr*, 1956, no. 10, 180.*

151.   Unsigned report,'Dramaturg-skazochnik, *Smena*, 20 October
1956*; unsigned report, '60-letie Evgeniya Shvartsa', *Literaturnaya
gazeta*, 25 October 1956.*

152.   Quoted by V. Ketlinskaya in *My znali Evgeniya Shvartsa*, 102.

153.   M. Yankovskii, *Leningradskii Teatr komedii*, 124.

with 'minor themes' (154). Such accusations in these
times, fortunately, carried much less weight than they
would have ten years previously; in the forties they
would have represented an unanswerable condemnation.

> Some reviewers practise a very simple method
> of knocking comedy down - a simplified re-
> telling of the content ... Not long ago Fedor
> Panferov in *Literatura i zhizn'* retold Evgenii
> Shvarts's *The Tale of a Young Couple* in just
> this way, but none the less by no means
> convinced me that the education of our young
> people and the setting up of a family are
> trivial themes (155).

Once staged, the play spread quickly. It appeared
at the Central Transport Theatre in Moscow at the end of
January 1958 and had reached the Ivanov State Russian
Drama Theatre in Odessa a few months later (première
17 April 1958). It was also running at the Omsk Drama
Theatre in July 1963 and had been shown in no less than
five separate productions in East Germany by 1962 (156).
The play came out in two editions in 1958, as well as in
each of the three editions of collected plays.

Written later than, but performed before, *The Tale
of a Young Couple*, *The Ordinary Miracle* was a return to
the adults' fairy-tale genre, following the post-war
period of Shvarts's withdrawal. This play is not based
on Russian, or indeed on any specific, folklore tradition,
but is more like a costume-piece comedy of manners with
one or two magic circumstances. Unlike Shvarts's other
main fairy-tales, *The Ordinary Miracle* is not a political
fairy-tale, but a rather sentimental love story, with
some elements of social satire.

The plot concerns a Magician who has married an
ordinary human wife and promised to settle down, but
cannot resist occasional exhibitions of magic, even if
it is only to put four legs on all the chickens and
moustaches on the hens. In just such a creative mood, we

154. N. Akimov, 'Trudnosti i perspektivy zhanra' (speech at an
editorial meeting of the journal *Oktyabr'*, 6 May 1958), in his
O teatre, 219.

155. Ibid.

156. *Teatr*, 1958, no. 3, 174; Poster, TsGALI, fond 2215, opis' 1,
ed. khr. 308, list 6; *Teatr*, 1963, no. 7, 134*; A. Dymshits in
My znali Evgeniya Shvartsa, 167.

learn, he once changed a young bear into a man, with the
condition that he will not be freed until a princess
falls in love with him and kisses him. The Magician's
wife is shocked when she meets the Bear and hears the
story, and even more horrified when her husband tells her
he has so arranged it that they are about to receive a
visit from a king with a daughter. Naturally, the
Princess and the Bear meet and fall in love, but when she
introduces him to her father and the court and announces
her intention of kissing him, he runs away in terror, for
he realises that he does not want to be released from the
spell if it means losing her. The Princess, ignorant of
the spell, angry at the whole world and the Bear, dresses
as a boy and rides away to live her own life.

The second act takes place in a mountain inn, where
the Magician has contrived to bring together the Bear,
the Princess (masquerading as the pupil of a famous huntsman), and the King and his court. He has also arranged
for a blizzard to imprison them in the inn, in the hope
that this will produce a solution to the problem. The
Bear and the Princess meet and recognise each other, but
not until the Princess is about to marry the King's Chief
Administrator in a fit of pique does the Bear explain
exactly why he cannot marry her. At this she is no longer
angry but, unable to see a way out of the tangle, she runs
away again, and the scene ends on a very gloomy note.

The final act takes place in the King's palace,
where the Princess is once again preparing to marry the
Chief Administrator, who has almost taken over the king-
dom. However, the Princess is pining for the Bear and
feels that she is slowly dying. Finally, the Bear arrives
and, after a reconciliation, she kisses him, whereupon the
'ordinary miracle' takes place, and he remains human. As
the Magician explains: 'Love has so completely recast him
that he can never become a bear again' (*OM*, 507).

As mentioned above, this play is not set in any
specific folklore context. In fact, Shvarts appears to
be deliberately aiming at a universal setting, for none
of the major characters has a name to betray his or her
origin and the 'traditional' characters are all fairly
atypical. The plot turns on a magic spell; but magic,
having once created the situation, is then powerless to
resolve it and retreats into the background, leaving the
characters themselves to work out the solution. As a
result, 'fairy-tale logic' is not very evident in this
play, except for the obvious example of turning an animal
into a human, rather than vice versa, of which A. Kron
observed that 'no teller of fairy-tales thought of that
before ... but, after all, it is no less plausible' (a

very typical reaction to this form of logic) (157).
Satire in this play is on a limited level, and is present in only three characters - the King, the Chief
Administrator and the Huntsman. The King is equated in
the play's prologue with an 'ordinary domestic tyrant'
(although 'in the fairy tale he is made a king so that
the features of his character can be carried to a logical conclusion'), who bullies everyone and blames his
bad temper on various causes (OM, 437-8). Indeed,
except towards his beloved daughter, he is very unpre-
dictable, his moods ranging from joviality to attempted
murder in the space of a few minutes. He knows very well
that he is wicked, but he has found a scapegoat - his
ancestors. As a result, he deeply regrets the necessity
for evil-doing, but says he cannot help it. 'My
ancestors', he complains,

> behaved like pigs in their own lifetime, and
> I have to answer for it ... By nature I'm a
> good chap, intelligent ... and then I go and
> do such awful things it makes me want to cry ...
> I'm a well-read, conscientious man. Anyone
> else would blame his meanness on his friends,
> his boss, his neighbours, his wife. But I
> blame my ancestors, since they're dead. It
> makes no difference to them, and it makes me
> feel better. (OM, 446-7)

This speech echoes an earlier one, written by Shvarts
for the King in one of the early drafts of *The Naked
King*, where he says:

> I am an egoist ... It's a purely monarchical
> disease. It's not a nice thing, lads. Because
> of this blasted egoism we murder our own brothers,
> we poison our aunts. And not only relatives -
> we attack complete strangers ... And there's
> nothing I can do about it ... (158)

This unwillingness to take responsibility for their own
actions is characteristic of many of Shvarts's more
comic villains.

The Chief Administrator is a cynical, ruthless
career bureaucrat, who tyrannises over the court in various petty ways. He represents the essence of centralism,

157. *'Obyknovennoe chudo'*, *Teatr*, 1956, no. 5, 111.

158. *'Golyi korol'* ... Avtograf', TsGALI, fond 2215, opis' 1,
ed. khr. 7, list 96.

to the extent of being displeased when the court ladies
use their initiative and have a wash after a long journey: 'If you are going to go around washing, over my head,
I must decline to take any further responsibility. Some
kind of order must be preserved, ladies' (*OM*, 458). Finally, he takes advantage of his engagement to the Princess to call himself the 'Administrative Prince' and to
patronise the King, calling him 'our kingling'. The
fact that the King puts up with this in itself reveals
the extent to which the Administrator has risen, since
the King has just threatened to execute the Prime Minister for calling him 'not the greatest of all kings,
but only a prominent king, that's all' (*OM*, 500). The
habit of putting people into categories and treating
them accordingly is a point which Shvarts had ridiculed
before in *The Shadow*, where the Majordomo tells the servant how many iced buns should be given to people of
various ranks. This kind of hierarchical distribution is
universal, and Shvarts was well-acquainted with the
Soviet variety, as shown by his account of the distribution of cabins on a river steamer in the course of a
writers' trip in the thirties. The distribution was
obviously made by some petty-bureaucratic relative of the
Prime Minister, while a forerunner of the King was among
the writers, for Shvarts related:

> He solemnly and publicly allotted single berths to
> great writers, twin berths to prominent writers,
> and disposed of the rest into shared cabins. One
> of the prominent writers was terribly offended
> and tried to get in as a great, but he was
> rejected. (159)

The third main source of satire is the famous
Huntsman who has killed much game in his day, but for
some time now has been too occupied with preserving his
reputation from criticism to do any hunting. Besides,
having gained various diplomas to prove he is famous, he
is now afraid of falling from these heights: 'Those below will start criticising each of my shots – I'd go mad!
They'd say: he killed that fox the same way as last
year; he's not bringing anything new to the art of hunting' (*OM*, 469). The Huntsman, in fact, is a classic
example of unproductive professional jealousy.

The Ordinary Miracle is accorded somewhat undeserved
praise by the Soviet critics – perhaps because of its
somewhat sentimental lyrical romanticism and elements of

---

159. Quoted by Slonimskii in *My znali Evgeniya Shvartsa*, 20.

Soviet satire, which would appeal to the Russian mind.
It has, however, a somewhat wordily-expressed and rambl-
ing plot, and as a fairy-tale it is a lesser play than
the other fairy-tales for adults, having too diffuse a
negative side. There is no one major villain, but there
are a few minor ones, whose negative characteristics
have very little to do with the main plot. However, it
is precisely with regard to the 'villains' that the play
presents one of its most interesting features.

All Shvarts's previous major fairy-tales for adults
had been on themes taken from international politics -
capitalist Europe and Nazism - and had contained satire,
sometimes exclusively directed at those targets and sometimes of a more general nature, equally applicable to
'survivals from the past' within the Soviet system itself. Here, for the first time, in *The Ordinary Miracle*,
there is no particular reference to international affairs;
the tale is, as mentioned above, carefully kept out of
any context and given a modern tone; thus what satire
there is automatically becomes of less 'universal' than
specifically Soviet application in the minds of Soviet
spectators. Indeed, in the prologue, such characters
as the King and the Administrator are explicitly linked
with their counterparts in everyday Soviet life. To
contemplate such a play would not have been possible until
after the death of Stalin, and actually to stage if required a climate such as that of 1956.

According to V. Smirnova, *The Ordinary Miracle* was
begun in the summer of 1953, a time which she said was
for Shvarts a 'period of enforced "calm" - one of his
plays was "not getting through", and there were publication problems as well ...' (160). None the less there
was a noticeable relaxation of pressure following the
death of Stalin, and Shvarts seems to have felt that perhaps he could at last return to his own unique genre of
Soviet fairy-tales for adults. His friend Akimov seemed
to think so too, for at some stage in 1953 he wrote an
article about the definition of the term 'Soviet play',
which included a brief apologia for the fairy-tale (in
the context of the adult theatre, since no mention was
made of children's drama) (161).

160. 'Skazochnik na teatre', 246.

161. N. Akimov, 'O bol'shikh vozmozhnostyakh i nebol'shikh
nedorazumeniyakh', 1953, first published in his *O teatre*, 1962, 27.

Should we not agree that we consider a Soviet
play to be any play which brings us Soviet
ideas, whatever narrative form the author may
have chosen for this? That a Soviet view of
history can be expressed on stage only in a
Soviet play? That Soviet ideas expressed in
the form of a fairy-tale make that fairy-tale
a Soviet one? (162)

The first minor thaw of 1953 soon lost impetus and
was already over when *The Ordinary Miracle* was finished
in 1954. Nevertheless, some ground had been gained and
the situation must have appeared hopeful, for in October
1954 it was reported in *Teatr* that G. Tovstonogov (who
had worked with the Comedy Theatre during Akimov's
absence) was now working with the Leningrad Komsomol
Theatre on Shvarts's *The Bear (Medved')* - a name which the
play bore, at least in parentheses, right up until its
appearance on stage (163).

In February 1955 the play was still 'in the
theatre's repertoire plan', but no more was subsequently
heard of the project (164). Not until the following year
was *The Ordinary Miracle* finally produced on stage, but
when it did appear, it came out in both Moscow and Leningrad within a few months.

The first production was in Moscow - in the Film-
actors' Studio Theatre, with Shvarts's friend and collab-
orator E. Garin directing (in conjunction with Kh.
Lokshina) and playing the role of the King. The Moscow
production probably began in January, and the Leningrad
production in the Comedy Theatre began three months later
(première on 30 April 1956) (165).

Both productions provoked a considerable reaction
in the press, and Shvarts mentioned the number of letters
and newspaper cuttings he himself had received, from
friends and strangers alike, in connection with the
play (166). Most of the reactions were favourable,

162. Ibid, 27.

163. *Teatr*, 1954, no. 10, 161.*

164. *Teatr*, 1955, no. 2, 161.*

165. The poster in the TsGALI file (fond 2215, opis' 1, ed. khr.
306, list 1) mentions Moscow showings on 18, 21, 22, 24 and 26
January 1956, but refers to the production not as a première, but
as a 'new production' - the next stage of novelty.

166. Letter to E. Garin and Kh. Lokshina, 17 May 1956, quoted by
Garin in *My znali Evgeniya Shvartsa*, 221.

although some critics raised objections to the roles of the Bear and the Princess, saying that their characters were ill-defined and that they were too passive (167). Other criticisms were levelled at the uneven quality of the play (168).

One of the most significant points about *The Ordinary Miracle* is its place in the re-establishment of the fantastic element in the theatre. In Moscow, for example, the revivals of *The Bath-house* and *The Bed-bug (Klop)*, in 1953 and 1955 respectively, were joined later in the decade by the production of *The Ordinary Miracle* and the revivals of *Mystery Bouffe (Misteriya-Buff)* (1957) and *The Shadow* (1958). V. Diev in 1968 mentioned the resuscitation of Mayakovskii and added: 'The ever-strengthening position of fantasy on the boards of our stage is also demonstrated by the attention paid by various theatres to the drama of Evg. Shvarts' (169).

When *The Ordinary Miracle* came out, despite the precedent set by *The Bath-house* and *The Bed-bug*, the acceptance of the fantastic was by no means guaranteed, and various critics felt called upon to justify the play's existence. Among these was M. Zharov, who, although conceding a small point to possible opponents, was none the less definitely in support of the genre:

> Of course, in both its theme and its genre this production does not lie on the main path of development of Soviet theatrical art, but if the assertion is justified that we need 'good and varied' works, then the production of *The Ordinary Miracle* has every right to exist. (170)

I. Kvasnetskaya, too, despite criticism of the play's weak points concluded that 'Obviously it is time for a return to the stage of that undeservedly rejected genre - the fairy-tale for adults' (171). Indeed, her article is conspicuously entitled 'In defence of a genre'.

167. For example: M. Kvasnetskaya, 'V zashchitu zhanra', *Moskovskii komsomolets*, 20 June 1956; M. Zharov, *'Obyknovennoe chudo'*, *Sovetskaya kul'tura*, 22 May 1956, 2. Both articles refer to the Moscow production.

168. For example: A. Karaganov, 'Dva spektaklya Leningradskogo teatra komedii', *Sovetskaya kul'tura*, 18 October 1956, 3; and see also Kvasnetskaya's article, quoted in footnote 167.

169. 'Problema uslovnosti', in A.O. Boguslavskii, V.A. Diev, eds., *Russkaya sovetskaya dramaturgiya*, III, 1946-1966, M., 1968, 172.

170. *'Obyknovennoe chudo'*, *Sovetskaya kul'tura*, 22 May 1956, 2.

171. 'V zashchitu zhanra', *Moskovskii komsomolets*, 20 June, 1956.

Perhaps something of this attitude governed Akimov's treatment of the Comedy Theatre production. In 1972 M. Zhezhelenko quoted a complaint, made by I. Solov'eva in 1956, that the theatre's Moscow summer tour (*The Ordinary Miracle* and Priestley's *Dangerous Corner*) lacked the 'novelty of the director's self-revelation' which had characterised Akimov's 1954 offering (with another theatre): Sukhovo-Kobylin's *The Lawsuit (Delo)* (172). However, Zhezhelenko suggested in Akimov's defence that the similarity between *The Ordinary Miracle* and former productions such as the 1940 *Shadow* was deliberate rather than coincidental. 'After all ... [Akimov] was dismissed from the Comedy Theatre precisely as a director who was excessively keen on theatricality and irony on stage. Now Akimov was taking his revenge and wanted to win a victory on the old battlefield' (173). This explanation is quite plausible, as such an attitude would be very much in Akimov's style.

Shvarts himself was well aware of the difficulties involved in the staging of such a play, after so many years of strictly orthodox drama, capable of only one interpretation and containing no elements of satire on Soviet society. In his letter to Garin and Lokshina, co-directors of the Moscow production, he wrote: 'Erast [Garin] has made a production out of a play I didn't even believe in myself. That is, I didn't believe that it would be possible to stage it' (174).

A measure of Shvarts's doubts about the reception of the play by an unaccustomed audience is the fact that he considered it necessary to write a statement of intent, originally as a kind of programme note, which has since been published and spoken as a prologue to the play. It was treated as a verbal introduction by the Comedy Theatre in the Leningrad production, which elicited a criticism from one commentator, A. Kochetov, who despite his general approval recommended that the theatre should omit the prologue, 'which to a considerable degree discloses the content of the play, and thereby detracts from the sharpness of the audience's perception of the action' (175). Kochetov pointed out that the Moscow production was having equal success without any such introduction. On this subject Shvarts himself wrote to his friend, L. Malyugin:

172. I. Solov'eva, 'Dvinutsya dal'she vpered', *Sovetskaya Rossiya*, 4 October 1956, 3; cited in Zhezhelenko, *Portrety rezhisserov*, book 1, 68.

173. Zhezhelenko, 'Akimov', in *Portrety rezhisserov*, book 1, 68.

174. Quoted by Garin in *My znali Evgeniya Shvartsa*, 221.

175. 'Veselaya p'esa-skazka', *Vechernii Leningrad*, 2 June 1956, 3.

> I had written something for the programme,
> a kind of libretto. In it I said that one
> should not look for hidden meanings in a
> fairy-tale, because the tale is told, not
> to hide, but to reveal one's thoughts ...
> The theatre did not, after all, print the
> programme with these explanations, but none
> the less the audience can usually make sense
> of a play without a guidebook. Usually. (176)

Both productions of *The Ordinary Miracle* continued
for some time. The sixtieth performance in Moscow was
timed to coincide with Shvarts's sixtieth birthday (177).
The play was still in the theatre's repertoire in December 1958, while the Comedy Theatre's production was
mentioned in a review in July 1959 (178). Although it
did not begin to spread as quickly as *The Tale of a
Young Couple*, but apparently waited until the next period
of relative freedom in 1959, by the end of the fifties
and during the sixties the play was being produced
throughout the Soviet Union, in a manner unparalleled by
The Shadow, *The Dragon* and *The Naked King*, which were
apparently confined to the two capitals. In July 1959
The Ordinary Miracle was being performed in the Barnaul
Youth Theatre (179). July 1962 saw a production by the
students of the Nemirovich-Danchenko studio of the Moscow
Art Theatre (180). In 1963 the play was being performed
by the Omsk Youth Theatre and was in preparation in the
Griboedov Theatre in Tbilisi (181). In that year it even
reached the repertoire list in *Teatr*, totalling 106 performances and being produced in seven theatres simultaneously (182). In 1966 there was another production by
theatrical students, this time in the School of Directing
at the State Institute of Theatrical Art, and in January
1971 the Satire Theatre began a production which lasted
at least until 1975 (183).

176. Quoted by Malyugin in *My znali Evgeniya Shvartsa*, 114.

177. Poster for production, '21 Oct. 1956. For the author's 60th
birthday ... for the 60th time'; TsGALI, fond 2215, opis' 1,
ed. khr. 306, list 12.*

178. L. Makovkin, 'Esli smotret' na skazku kak na skazku',
Vechernii Sverdlovsk, 16 July 1959, 3 (report and criticism of
Comedy Theatre on tour).

179. *Altaiskaya pravda*, 25 July 1959.*

180. A. Sherel', 'Diplomnye spektakli. Chto oni obeshchayut',
Moskovskii komsomolets, 7 July 1962, 3.

181. *Teatr*, 1963, no. 2, 117*; *Teatr*, 1963, no. 7, 133.*

182. *Teatr*, 1964, no. 8, 91.*

183. *Teatr*, 1966, no. 12, 135*; M.Ya. Linetskaya (comp.)
Moskovskii Teatr Satiry (al'bom), M., 1974.

A film was made in 1964 which apparently took considerable liberties with the original (184). There was also a radio broadcast of the Comedy Theatre production (185). There is even a musical comedy version with music by V. Grokhovskii which was in the repertoire of the Ivanovo Musical Comedy Theatre when it came on tour to Moscow in the summer of 1975. Apart from the three editions of the collected plays, the work was also published in a small collection shortly after its appearance on stage in 1956 (186).

The Ordinary Miracle holds a relatively minor place in the hierarchy of Shvarts's plays, at least as seen through Western eyes. Tsimbal, however, called it 'one of [Shvarts's] most profound fairy-tales', perhaps because it was not prompted by any events of international political significance, but was concerned, like much of the Thaw literature, with personal matters concerning individual people - albeit kings, princesses and magicians (187). Certainly as a means of publicising Shvarts's fairy-tales for adults throughout the Soviet Union it has had considerable significance.

Between 1929 and 1958 Evgenii Shvarts wrote more than thirty plays, films and revues, of which only twenty-two appeared during his lifetime. Since his death, four more have been produced for the first time and others have increased their currency throughout the Soviet Union and abroad. In fact, Shvarts's fame, at least in the adult theatre, has been mainly acquired posthumously, owing to the unfortunate coincidence of his creative life with the era of Stalinism.

Shvarts's natural metier was, of course, the fairy-tale, whether for adults or for children. This genre not only enabled him to make statements which might otherwise have been suppressed, it was also the one best suited to his style of self-expression and his very rich imagination. An entry in Shvarts's diary illustrates his preference for fairy-tales as opposed to more realistic works.

184.   L. Pogozheva, 'Brak po lyubvi', *Iskusstvo kino*, 1965, no. 4, 14-17.

185.   Advance report, unplaced, undated, TsGALI, fond 2215, opis' 1, ed. khr. 332, list 16.*

186.   *Ten' i drugie p'esy*, L., 1956.

187.   *Evgenii Shvarts*, 221.

> No-one can resist the temptation to make it
> a little more touching here, more character-
> istic there, more significant somewhere else.
> When it enters literature, a phenomenon as
> such becomes simplified. It's much better
> to write fairy tales. You're not tied to
> verisimilitude, and yet it's more truthful. (188)

Sentimentality is sometimes present in Shvarts's fairy-
tales, but the risk of such melodrama as occasionally
mars his realistic plays is lessened by the fact that,
by definition, almost anything is natural in a fairy-
tale - within certain limits. With regard to these
limits, S. Dreiden quoted Shvarts as having said:

> The laws of reality in fairy-tales are different
> from those prevailing in real life, but none the
> less they are laws, and very strict ones. The
> events which take place in fairyland are very
> 'colourful', and such colour is one of the best
> features of the theatre. (189)

The concept of laws which must be obeyed in fairy-
tales was very important to Shvarts, and contributed
much to the inner unity of his fairy-tale plays.
Shvarts's words about Andersen in 1955 could equally
well apply to his own creations:

> His fairy-tales were nothing like those artificial,
> excessively magic ones, where even a miracle is no
> miracle because here anything can happen. His
> fairy-tale world was inseparably tied to the real
> world, to his own time, his people and his
> country. And in the world of his fairy-tales life
> went on according to the laws of nature, albeit
> the nature of fairy-tales. (190)

According to Dreiden, Shvarts also compared fairy-
tales to scientific experiments, where a subject is
placed in a certain kind of artificial environment (in
this case a magic one) in order to study its reactions
within that environment (191). The result, in Shvarts's
plays, is usually that the subject's reactions vary
from those common in the real world only to the extent

188. Extract from Shvarts's diary, 17 April 1942, in 'V dni
ispytanii', 230-1.

189. In introduction to Shvarts, *Kukol'nyi gorod. P'esy*, L., 1959,
21.

190. 'Tri chuda', 168.

191. In introduction to Shvarts, *Kukol'nyi gorod*, 15.

that the subject's world deviates from reality. This
law provides the basis, not only for Shvarts's use of
'fairy-tale logic', but also for many details of plot
and character in his plays. The story of *The Shadow*, for
example, is built on two assumptions. The first is a
variation from accepted reality - that a man's shadow can
leave him and exist apart from him. However, this licence
does not extend to allowing it to become a real human
being. It remains a shadow, bound to its master by un-
breakable ties. The second assumption follows naturally
from this condition - a headless man cannot have a complete shadow. Thus the ending of *The Shadow* is entirely
within the 'laws of ... the nature of fairy-tales' cited
by Shvarts.

Magic in Shvarts's plays, whether defined as the
product of boundless 'energy' *(The Adventures of Hohenstaufen)*, hailed as a miracle *(The Ordinary Miracle)*,
explained by a dream or (more usually) taken for granted,
is presented as a simple and even natural phenomenon.
Even in *The Adventures of Hohenstaufen* it is readily
acceptable, to such a degree that Boibabchenko, having
learnt the truth from Kofeikina, is shortly afterwards
able to explain it in turn to Hohenstaufen, ending com-
placently, 'It's a fairy-tale, that's all. You'd better
get used to it' *(AH, 50)*. In *The Ordinary Miracle* the
Magician rejoices at the 'miracle', but without much surprise, except that he himself did not anticipate such a
natural outcome: 'Look: he's a man, a man walking down
the path with his sweetheart ... What a complete fool I
am' *(OM, 507)*. A good definition of one type of magic
in Shvarts's work has been given by S. Babenysheva:

> Magic for him is what is possible, it is the
> good which lives in the human soul, and which
> people are not always able to express in real
> life ... In fairy-tales they become themselves,
> more so than in ordinary life. (192)

This definition, however, does not take into account the
'magic' at the disposal of the villains. The Dragon, for
example, is naturally not using 'the good that lives in
the human soul', but his magic is as much a form of self-
expression as is that of the heroes. In speaking of the
villains, one might reverse Babenysheva's statement, sub-
stituting 'evil' for 'good', or one can apply Shvarts's
own words from the prologue to *The Ordinary Miracle* -
that these are ordinary people, put into fairy-tales 'so
that the features of [their] character can be carried to
a logical conclusion'. *(OM, 438)*

192.   'Obyknovennoe i neobyknovennoe chudo', 250.

Shvarts's use of the fairy-tale genre was very traditional, in that he used allegory and caricature in order to 'express his dreams and get even with wickedness' (193). However, although his basic aims may have been traditional, his methods in dealing with the material at his disposal were not. Moreover, Shvarts used three different types of fairy-tale - the adaptations of existing works, those which he composed himself on the basis of general traditional material, and those other compositions which combined magic with modern reality. Each of these types required a different approach.

The task of adapting existing fairy-tales generally involved increasing the length by adding extra characters, providing more detailed characterisations and adding detail and incidents to the plot. Many fairy-tales, of both traditional and later origin, have plots which extend over considerable time and distance, but they almost invariably observe the unity of action. In his adaptations Shvarts tended to reverse this rule, tightening the unities of time and space, but varying the action considerably. This process is best seen in *The Shadow*.

Shvarts's adaptations usually incorporate a modern approach to the original. This contrasts with his methods when composing original plays from traditional material. In the adaptations the plot was a constant factor and therefore variety could be obtained by the means already described, as long as the main theme remained undisturbed. In the case of original compositions, however, there was no accepted plot to follow, and the constant factor was the folklore tradition itself. Therefore, such compositions needed to be firmly rooted in whatever tradition was chosen, or much of the effect would be lost. This is best illustrated in the children's plays, but *The Ordinary Miracle* also maintains a consistent atmosphere, even though it is that of a nineteenth-century costume-piece with occasional magic, rather than of any national tradition. *The Dragon* too, although by virtue of its status as a political allegory it is allowed considerable leeway in the matter of contemporary references, is a very Teutonic creation, except, of course, for Lancelot, the outsider, who is universal ('he is St George, he is Perseus, in every land he has a different name') (*D*, 365).

193. V. Smirnova, 'Skazochnik na teatre', 270.

However, the lack of any significant contemporary element in these plays does not mean that they are divorced from reality. Yu. Alyanskii wrote that if a fairy-tale did not have roots in the real world, 'then it would be not a fairy-tale but poor-quality fantasy', which Shvarts's plays are certainly not (194). In each play's message, in the characters – their speech, their actions and their reactions to each other – there is so much realism that specific echoes from the modern world are unnecessary.

The plays which combined magic and reality (the children's puppet plays, *The Adventures of Hohenstaufen* and *The Tale of a Young Couple*) required yet another approach. The proportion of reality to fantasy in these plays varies: from *The Tale of a Young Couple*, which is basically a realistic work, to the puppet play *Toy Town (Kukol'nyi gorod)*, which has only one 'ordinary' character; but the contemporary world plays a similar role in all of them. Here it is neither suppressed, as in the traditional compositions, nor merely allowed to break through occasionally, for effect, as in the adaptations. Instead it forms the basis for the fantasy and is taken for granted, even emphasised.

Fairy-tales were a particularly apt genre for Shvarts, not only because they suited his own inclination, but because through them he could express the official optimism of the Soviet regime without having to portray large numbers of model Soviet workers. As V. Smirnova wrote: 'The desire of the contemporary audience to see on stage positive and (most important) victorious heroes was easy for Shvarts to fulfil, because the fairy-tale has always demanded exactly the same thing' (195). Moreover, even in the heyday of the 'no-conflict theory', villains were always permissible, even indispensable, in fairy-tales.

By making his characters more detailed than is usual in fairy-tales, Shvarts gave motivation to actions which often seem arbitrary in traditional tales, and by this means also added to the point of the play. This is particularly obvious in the case of the villains. Traditional fairy-tale villains are inclined to be mere personifications of evil, and therefore potentially interchangeable, while the victory of the hero is one of abstract good over abstract evil. Shvarts's villains, on the other hand, all

194. 'Obyknovennyi volshebnik', 282.

195. 'Skazochnik na teatre', 261.

have an individual rationale of evil, a logical basis
for their particular type of villainy; and on that basis
they are defeated. The cold Snow Queen is vanquished by
warmth and friendship, the solitary autocratic Wolf in
Little Red Riding Hood is beaten by friendly collective
action, and the cynicism of the Dragon is overcome by the
practical idealism of Lancelot.

In the traditional conflict between good and evil,
the intentions of the characters are clearly defined,
partly for simplicity and partly from considerations of
length. However, Shvarts, whose fairy-tales are not
only longer but also considerably more subtle than the
traditional ones, allowed some half-tones of good and
evil. Thus, some of his characters are weak people,
easily swayed by other influences, such as Julia and the
Doctor in *The Shadow* or the townspeople in *The Dragon*;
while others are petty villains with occasional redeeming features, like Pietro in *The Shadow* or the King in
The Ordinary Miracle, both of whom are reluctantly devoted fathers.

From the point of view of the delivery of the message, there is a distinction between the methods Shvarts
used for his adults' and children's fairy-tales. The
children's plays are concerned with general abstract
themes and thus need only to be given a certain *emphasis*,
whereas the plays for adults set out to make a particular
point and must have a definite *direction*. Fairy-tales
and allegories, of course, are among the best media for
satire, and the complement of the positive themes involved
is satire against the villains. In the children's plays
it is aimed at abstracts such as laziness, greed and self-
ishness, while in the plays for adults it has a more
pointed application - either narrowed down to one particular person or referring to a specific category of
people.

Shvarts wrote six satires for adults, all with some
kind of fairy-tale status. They all show different
aspects of satire; the methods changed with the shift from
'reality' to true fantasy, and the targets changed according to the relative situations at home and abroad. The
Soviet satire on bad workers and bureaucracy to be found
in *The Telephone Receiver* and *The Adventures of Hohenstaufen* is based on situation comedy rather than on characterisation, and the method is a brief caricature,
followed by retribution and ridicule. In the true fairy-
tale plays caricature is less obvious, owing to the shortage of realistic standards against which to measure the
various characters. Moreover, the depth of characterisation increases between *The Naked King* and *The Ordinary
Miracle*.

In Shvarts's satirical plays, a surprising amount of the satire is directed at Soviet phenomena, even in works written during the Soviet period, such as *The Naked King* and *The Dragon*, which must have gained some degree of preliminary approval to have made even half the journey to the stage. I have in mind here not only exclusively 'Soviet' phenomena, but also various widespread occurrences such as careerism, bureaucracy and toadyism, which when presented to a Soviet audience would immediately evoke Soviet parallels. In fact, as in the case of *The Naked King* and *The Dragon*, 'Soviet satire' can be found even in the most direct 'anti-Western' references. *The Naked King*, in particular, was still embarrassingly topical after a quarter of a century. In this respect Shvarts's satire, like all good examples of the art, is widely applicable, time and place being of little account in the appreciation of the work.

Shvarts's choice of targets for satire indicates to a limited extent what topics, if any, were considered suitable at which times. However, since four out of the six satires for adults were not performed when they were written, and two of those four were never staged at all, the choice is more an indication of what Shvarts himself considered to be suitable. In fact, one of the most relevant questions to the discussion of the stage history of Shvarts's works is that of timing.

In the course of Shvarts's creative life, the literary and political situation changed many times, both for the better and for the worse. In many cases the success or failure of Shvarts's works in their Soviet context depended not so much on their literary quality as on the political and literary scene at the time of their appearance.

The Telephone Receiver and *The Adventures of Hohenstaufen*, for example, were written in the wake of such plays as *The Bed-bug*, *The Bath-house* and *Dear Comrade*, in which 'survivals from the past' were rebuked and ridiculed. The year 1929 had been a time of purges, but these were more widely publicised than later ones and were altogether more 'respectable', involving loss of position rather than loss of life. Thus they could safely be the subject of plays. By 1932, however, particularly after the April decree, such themes had been largely replaced by those of the five-year-plan, so that already such plays were a little untimely. The failure of *The Adventures of Hohenstaufen* may have been due to a combination of other circumstances - the unusual amount of fantasy, technical problems, closure of the Experimental Workshop - as well as ill-timing, but *The Telephone Receiver* would not have had such disadvantages.

By the mid-thirties it was no longer acceptable to write in detail about bad attitudes to work; the lightweight 'comedy of everyday life', with its accent on domestic matters, was the accepted genre for plays on Soviet themes. As the post-Kirov purges gathered momentum, and for twenty years thereafter, the only real possibility for satire was the sphere of international affairs, and the only legitimate target was the West. From this point of view, *The Naked King* was an eminently suitable offering, but the wholesale rejection of plays in 1936 was bound to include anything so obviously atypical. The rest of the thirties, for Shvarts, was devoted to realistic children's plays on topical themes, fairytales for children, and other harmless and definitely uncontroversial works, as the most suitable output in those evil times.

The 1940 production of *The Shadow* is a particularly good example of the importance of timing. There is evidence to suggest that 1940 was a period of relaxation of tension between the purges and the war. Apart from the appearance of *The Shadow*, there was also an article by the director Tairov in December 1940, noting the absence of Mayakovskii on the Soviet stage, and setting out his ideas for a new production of *The Bed-bug* for his Moscow Chamber Theatre. The article ends:

> Such is the general plan for the production.
> The first steps towards its realisation have
> been completed. In the Far East we have
> several times put on a 'concert' performance
> of *The Bed-bug* ... Now the troupe is working
> hard on the final version of the production.
> In a few months' time we intend showing the
> results of our work in Moscow. (196)

Of course, nothing came of this project, but the fact that it was begun at all testifies to some kind of change in the atmosphere at that time. Perhaps the appearance of *The Shadow* earlier in the year encouraged Tairov to attempt this production. *The Bed-bug*, however, because of its purely Soviet application would have been a much more dubious prospect than the largely anti-Western *The Shadow*.

Akimov's reluctance to advertise the prospective production of Shvarts's play until the last moment indicates that he was dubious about the outcome and indeed, had the attempt been made a year (or even a few months) earlier, it might easily have come to nothing. The

196. A. Tairov, 'Mayakovskii na stsene', *Teatr*, 1940, no. 12, 63.

evidence of the 1938 Akimov portrait of Shvarts gives
scope for speculation that the play was indeed written
earlier, but that either voluntarily or of necessity it
was held back for some time until the more favourable
literary climate emerged.

A further indication of the more temperate climate
is the recognition by various approving critics of the
Soviet applications of some of the satire. 'Survivals
from the past' had been dealt with faithfully in earlier
years, but by the late thirties the villains were the
more dangerous 'enemies of the people', while 'survivals
from the past' were generally considered to have been
outgrown. Thus, it is significant to find that not only
did Akimov refer in his exposition of the play to
'topical everyday themes, worthy of our satire', but other
critics also noted that 'such people can be found even
amongst ourselves' and referred to 'psychological characteristics, instilled into people by capitalism ...
survivals ... in the consciousness of Soviet people' (197).
Moreover, such references passed without comment, and the
play was not attacked as a slander.

The war was one of the most prolific periods of
Shvarts's creative life, although not everything he wrote
then was produced at the time. The early version of *The
Tale of a Young Couple* was rejected as being too personal
(worse still, it did not even deal with the war). The
timing of *The Dragon* was particularly unfortunate. Had it
appeared earlier (almost anything with a patriotic slant
was sure of success in the first years of the war), had
the attempt been made anywhere but in conservative Moscow,
the story might have been different, although *The Dragon*
was, of course, doubtful material at any stage of the
Stalin era.

The barrenness of the post-war period has already
been noted, as has Shvarts's reaction to it. Even the
relatively harmless *The Tale of a Young Couple* could not
have had a worse time chosen for its second attempt at
staging in 1949. The situation between then and 1953 was
even worse. Not only was Shvarts writing very little;
few of his plays were being performed, and many were under
attack.

197. N. Akimov, 'Skazka na nashei stsene', in his *O teatre*, 243;
I. L'vov, 'Skazka dlya vzroslykh', *Iskusstvo i zhizn'*, 1940, no. 5,
31; 'Skazka dlya vzroslykh', *Literaturnyi sovremennik*, 1940, no. 5-6,
229.

Only after the death of Stalin did conditions become at all favourable for new plays, such as *The Ordinary Miracle*, and for further attempts to stage previously rejected works. The Thaw, for Shvarts, became noticeable in 1954, with Tovstonogov's project to stage *The Ordinary Miracle*. 1956 saw the two successful productions of this play, and by the time *The Tale of a Young Couple* and *The Shadow* had finally reached the stage in 1957 and 1958, the 'rehabilitation' of Shvarts was well under way. The process was at first rapid, and reached its highest point in the early sixties, when approximately half his thirty-odd works were current in various forms. Since then, allowing for difficult periods, such as 1963 and 1968, Shvarts's popularity has been slowly consolidated by the gradual spread of his works and the appearance of films, operettas, radio productions and so on, based on the plays. A certain amount of vulgarisation is inherent in many of these productions made 'after Shvarts' (Shvarts's daughter has a low opinion of all the films made after his death), but they are at least indicative of an increasing awareness of Shvarts's unique place in Soviet drama.

One very noteworthy aspect of Shvarts's career was his constant close collaboration with people who appreciated his work and who were prepared to make the necessary effort to produce a result. While the average time-server could write plays suitable for any theatre, Shvarts's work was for a more exclusive clientèle. He wrote plays for a few specific theatres and made films with a select group of directors and actors. This pattern is a rare one in Soviet adult theatre. Bulgakov's association with the Moscow Art Theatre may be cited (although Shvarts's relations with the Comedy Theatre were noticeably better than Bulgakov's with 'his' troupe). Other writers mentioned in connection with the Comedy Theatre as being 'one of us', such as V. Shkvarkin, are also not in quite the same category, since their works spread rapidly to other theatres, which Shvarts's plays for adults at first did not. Indeed, during the thirties and forties, while critics were bitterly lamenting the lack of collaboration between theatres and playwrights, Shvarts was providing a perfect example of the principle - an example, unfortunately, in many cases little appreciated by the authorities.

The most significant member of Shvarts's theatrical *côterie* was, of course, Akimov, who was the playwright's most energetic supporter. According to Yankovskii, 'On [Shvarts's] own admission it was his meeting with Akimov which brought him into the adult theatre' (198). Having once led Shvarts to write plays for adults, Akimov continued to exhort, encourage and defend him with an enthusiasm which took little account of unfavourable conditions. Writing about the production of *The Shadow*, Tsimbal noted that it was by no means Akimov's first attempt to stage a Shvarts play, but that so far none had succeeded; he added: 'and so there must have been real mutual confidence between the playwright and the director, in order to have continued their creative collaboration' (199). This is a very sound comment. In the course of Shvarts's life relatively few of his plays were accepted without any problems, and only one or two of his plays for adults were not initially blocked from the stage by some obstacle or other. Of those children's plays which disappeared without trace before the première, none returned, but four out of the seven plays for adults which suffered major setbacks at the first attempt were later brought back; of these resurrections two (*The Dragon* and *The Tale of a Young Couple*) were effected by Akimov, and one — the blockade play *One Night (Odna noch')* — by the Comedy Theatre after his death. Akimov and Shvarts had very similar methods of self-expression, whether in speaking and writing or through the theatre, and Tsimbal was not exaggerating when he later referred to Akimov's 'truly fanatical belief in Shvarts's dramatic vocation' (200).

Another question which could be raised is that of Soviet literary criticism as applied to Shvarts. This has been of two types: contemporary criticism, associated with the appearance of specific plays, and the more general appraisals, covering several plays at once, which have become more common of recent years.

During the thirties and forties, the majority of Shvarts's plays (that is, of those which were staged) met with approval from most critics when they first appeared. This was partly due to the fact that appearance on stage is in itself a guarantee of some degree of official approval, and that after 1932 the amount of literary polemic decreased sharply.

198. *Leningradskii Teatr komedii*, 48.

199. 'Poiski komedii', *Literaturnaya gazeta*, 10 May 1940.

200. 'Mudraya predannost' teatru', *Teatr*, 1969, no. 4, 49.

Considering the nature of much Stalinist literary criticism, it is surprising that the concept of 'formalism' was invoked so rarely in connection with Shvarts's work. After the rout of genuine Formalism in 1930 the word acquired a whole range of meanings, few of which bore any relation to real Formalism, and all of which could be translated as 'bad'. Anything out of the ordinary was liable to be stigmatised as 'formalist' and perhaps Shvarts was saved only by the fact that those of his plays which actually reached the stage between 1936 and 1940 were all in recognised genres and conspicuous only by their quality. However, criticism of the unstaged plays was equally restrained from this point of view, probably because the real witch-hunters of the period never encountered these works. Yankovskii, in a very tolerant spirit, applied the term formalist to *The Adventures of Hohenstaufen*, but did not make a point of the accusation. In general, Shvarts survived the formalist-baiting of the thirties without problems. In the forties, however, he was not so lucky. The attacks on the 'bourgeois formalism' of the 'cosmopolitans' left him largely unscathed, but the use of *The Shadow* as ammunition in the attacks on the Comedy Theatre was quickly followed by accusations condemning the 'formalism' of his puppet plays. Nevertheless, Shvarts does seem to have been let off comparatively lightly in this matter, particularly in view of his suspect 'German' name.

The criticism as well as the production of Shvarts's plays involved a limited circle of people. It is interesting that those critics who habitually reviewed Shvarts's plays were those who, in general, approved of him. In most cases an unfavourable opinion from such critics, if occasionally undeserved, was expressed in very restrained terms, and more with regret that the play concerned was not up to the usual standard than as any form of attack. Attacks, when they did come, were from people with a political point to make, who chose to deal with Shvarts at that time because that play was a suitable target for their arguments. The names of critics like S. Borodin did not recur in connection with Shvarts, but vanished with the end of their own particular campaign. Thus, there was no habitual opposition to Shvarts, but there was habitual approval for his works. The opposition was at times most expressive in its silent neglect. I. Shtok, writing of Shvarts's problems during the Stalinist era, claimed: 'They banned his works. They slated him in newspapers and journals. They wrecked his plays on purpose, to show that he was untalented. Even such tactics as these were practised' (201). But if Shvarts had problems

---

201. I. Shtok, 'Evgenii Shvarts', in his *Rasskazy o dramaturgakh*, 146.

with the critics, he also posed some problems for them.
As the film director G. Kozintsev wrote:

> During his lifetime, they could never find the
> right label for him ... They tried to consider
> him just a children's writer, but his characters
> made the adults think, too. They reproached him
> because some of his plots were repetitions of
> Andersen, but 'even Shakespeare used other
> people's stories' ... They picked at him for
> departing from reality (who needs fairy-tales
> nowadays?) and for coming too close to reality
> (they're fairy-tales, but they're just like
> real life!) (202)

In more recent years, the criticism devoted to
Shvarts's work in general has a tendency to disregard or
dismiss all but a few of the plays. This tendency
reached its most extreme form perhaps in E. Min's review
of the 1960 collected edition, in which half the space
was devoted to the children's tale *The Snow Queen* and the
other half to *The Shadow*, while of the other eight works
in the book, *The Dragon* was mentioned twice and *The Ordinary Miracle* and another of the children's fairy-tales
once each.

Evgenii Shvarts died on 15 January 1958 at the age
of sixty-one. His obituary appeared in *Literaturnaya
gazeta* on 18 January, signed by thirty-five friends,
including colleagues such as Akimov, Kozintsev and N.
Cherkasov, and other well-known literary names such as
O. Berggol'ts, D. Granin and V. Panova. The obituary
mentioned the names of eight of his works – a poor tally
out of the thirty-odd which he actually completed – presumably representing those which were being performed at
the time of his death.

The formal phrases of an official obituary do not
necessarily make the best epitaph, and a better contemporary comment on Shvarts and his work is probably that
found as a mere passing reference in an article by Akimov,
a few months later (203). The article dealt mainly with
fantasy and imagination as assets to the theatre, paying
particular attention to E. Vakhtangov and his last and
most spectacular production, *Princess Turandot* (1922).

202. *Glubokii ekran*, M., 1971, 203.

203. 'Prazdnik na stsene', *Leningradskaya pravda*, 27 May 1958.

In connection with this, Akimov paid tribute to Shvarts's
unique place in Soviet theatre: 'Perhaps only Evgenii
Shvarts, in his fairy-tales for the stage, has managed
to keep alive until today the principles of Vakhtangov's
discovery, the secret of creating a festival of
theatrical pageantry' (204).

204. Ibid.

BIBLIOGRAPHY

This does not claim to be a full bibliography on Shvarts and his fairy-tales for adults. I have included only those items quoted in the present work. A fuller bibliography on Shvarts and his plays can be found in my unpublished M.A. thesis, 'Yevgenii Shvarts and his drama', Australian National University, Canberra, 1977, on which this monograph is based.

L.=Leningrad, M.=Moscow.

Archival Materials

Items are given in the order: *fond/opis'/ed.khr.*

2215/1/7 (1934). *The Naked King* (typed copy and manu-script draft section).

2215/1/17 (1943). *The Dragon* (typed copy with Shvarts's and Akimov's annotations).

2215/1/306 (1956-58). Programmes and posters for two productions of *The Ordinary Miracle*.

2215/1/308 (1957-58). Programmes and posters for three productions of *The Tale of a Young Couple*.

2215/1/312 (1961-62). Programmes and poster for two productions of *The Dragon*.

2215/1/322 (1929-61). Articles relating to productions of various plays by Shvarts, including *The Dragon*.

2215/1/327 (1940-62). Articles about various productions of *The Shadow*.

2215/1/332 (1956-62). Articles about various productions of *The Ordinary Miracle*.

Other Materials

Aikhenval'd, Yu., 'Perekhodnyi vozrast', *Teatr*, 1970, no. 2, 51-7.

Akimov, N., 'Ne budem narushat' uslovii igry', *Rabochii i teatr*, 1935, no. 13, 6-7.

Akimov, N., 'O printsipakh igry', *Iskusstvo i zhizn'*, 1940, no. 1, 20.

Akimov, N., 'O putyakh myuzik-kholla', *Rabochii i teatr*, 1934, no. 17, 5-7.

Akimov, N., *O teatre*, L., 1962.

Akimov, N., 'Prazdnik na stsene', *Leningradskaya pravda*, 27 May 1958.

Akimov, N., 'Uverennost'', *Literaturnaya gazeta*, 14 March 1963, 3.

Akimov, N., and others, 'E.L. Shvarts', *Literaturnaya gazeta*, 18 January 1958, 4.

Alyanskii, Yu., 'Obyknovennyi volshebnik', in his *Teatral'nye legendy*, M., 1973, 276-303.

Andersen, H.C., *Andersen's Fairy-Tales*, trans. Jean Hersholt, New York, 1942.

Andersen, H.C., *Andersen's Longer Stories*, trans. Jean Hersholt, New York, 1948.

Andersen, H.C., *Andersen's Shorter Tales*, trans. Jean Hersholt, New York, 1948.

Babenysheva, S., 'Obyknovennoe i neobyknovennoe chudo', *Novyi mir*, 1961, no. 2, 249-53.

Benyash, R., 'Efremov', in *Portrety rezhisserov*, book 1, M., 1972, 181-222.

Boguslavskii, A.O. and V.A. Diev, eds., *Russkaya sovetskaya dramaturgiya*, vol. III, 1946-1966, M., 1968.

Borev, Yu., 'Sotsialisticheskii realizm i drama-kontseptsiya', in N.K. Gei and others, eds., *Sotsialisticheskii realizm i khudozhestvennoe razvitie chelovechestva*, M., 1966, 398-426.

Borodin, S., 'Vrednaya skazka', *Literatura i iskusstvo*,

25 March 1944, 3.

Campbell, A.J.C., 'Plays and Playwrights', *Survey*, January, 1963, 68-76.

Chamisso, A., *Peter Schlemihl, the Shadowless Man*, trans. Joseph Jacobs, London, n.d.

Corten, I.H.S., 'Evgenij Švarc: Man and artist', Ph.D. thesis, Berkeley University, 1972.

Deich, A., 'Dva spektaklya Teatra komedii', *Moskovskii bol'shevik*, 26 May 1940.

Ernst, C., 'Die Furchtsamkeit der Macht', *Der Kurier*, 5 April 1947.

Etkind, M., *N.P. Akimov - khudozhnik*, L., 1960.

Golovashenko, Yu., 'Chelovek i ten'', *Vechernii Leningrad*, 14 December 1960, 3.

Golovchiner, V., 'Put' k skazke E. Shvartsa', in *Sbornik trudov molodykh uchenykh*, Tomsk, 1971, 170-85.

Grinberg, I., 'Ten'. Prem'era v Teatre komedii', *Leningradskaya pravda*, 17 April 1940, 3.

Grinberg, I., 'Uchenyi i ego ten'', *Literaturnaya gazeta*, 10 May 1940.

Johnson, P., *Khrushchev and the Arts. The Politics of Soviet Culture 1962-64*, Cambridge, Mass., 1965.

Karaganov, A., 'Dva spektaklya Leningradskogo teatra komedii', *Sovetskaya kul'tura*, 18 October 1956, 3.

Kardin, V., 'Posle pervogo desyatiletiya', *Teatr*, 1966, no. 4, 18-33.

Kochetov, A., 'Veselaya p'esa-skazka', *Vechernii Leningrad*, 2 June 1956, 3.

Kozintsev, G., *Glubokii ekran*, M., 1971.

Kron, A., *'Obyknovennoe chudo'*, *Teatr*, 1956, no. 5, 111-12.

Kulikova, K., 'Dvadtsat' let spustya', *Leningradskaya pravda*, 25 November 1960, 3.

Kunin, M., 'Realisticheskaya skazka', *Sovetskoe slovo*, Berlin, 5 May 1947.

Kvasnetskaya, M., 'V zashchitu zhanra', *Moskovskii komsomolets*, 20 June 1956.

Lebedev, A., 'Skazka est' skazka', *Teatr*, 1968, no. 4, 38-44.

Levidov, M., 'Dramaturg i ego ten'', *Literaturnaya gazeta*, 10 June 1940, 5.

Linetskaya, M.Ya., comp., *Moskovskii Teatr Satiry (al'bom)*, M., 1974.

L.M., 'Im Zauberreich der alten Märchen', *Spandauer Volksblatt*, 9 April 1947, 2.

L'vov, I., 'Skazka dlya vzroslykh', *Iskusstvo i zhizn'*, 1940, no. 5, 30-2.

Makovkin, L., 'Esli smotret' na skazku kak na skazku', *Vechernii Sverdlovsk*, 16 July 1959, 3.

Markish, P., 'Ten'', *Pravda*, 26 May 1940, 6.

Min, E., 'Sovetskii skazochnik', in *Teatr i zhizn'. Sbornik teatral'no-kriticheskikh statei*, L., 1957, 82-100.

Moldavskii, D., 'Gospodin Drakon, Gerr Burgomistr i drugie', *Literatura i zhizn'*, 1 July 1962, 4.

Moldavskii, D., 'Poeticheskii i skazochnyi mir Evgeniya Shvartsa', *Nash sovremennik*, 1967, no. 3, 106-10.

Moldavskii, D., 'Puteshestvie v skazochnyi mir', *Leningradskaya pravda*, 16 September 1956.

Movshenson, A., 'Dve prem'ery v Teatre komedii', *Rabochii i teatr*, 1936, no. 12, 20.

My znali Evgeniya Shvartsa, comp. Z. Nikitina and L. Rakhmanov, ed. S. Tsimbal, L., 1966.

Nazarov, B. and O. Gridneva, 'K voprosu ob otstavanii dramaturgii i teatra', *Voprosy filosofii*, 1956, no. 5, 85-94.

Pogozheva, L., 'Brak po lyubvi', *Iskusstvo kino*, 1965, no. 4, 14-17.

Pyman, A., 'Yevgeniy Shvarts', introduction to *Three Plays*, Oxford, 1972, vii-xlviii.

R.M., 'Lichtspiele um einen Schatten', *Der Sozialdemokrat*,

11 April 1947.

Shabad, T., 'Modernists defy Leningrad Reds', *New York Times*, 20 March 1963, 5.

Sherel', A., 'Diplomnye spektakli. Chto oni obeshchayut', *Moskovskii komsomolets*, 7 July 1962, 3.

Shklovskii, V., 'O skazke', *Detskaya literatura*, 1940, no. 6, 1-4.

Shtein, A., *Povest' o tom, kak voznikayut syuzhety*, M., 1965.

Shtok, I., 'Evgenii Shvarts' in his *Rasskazy o dramaturgakh*, M., 1967, 138-48.

Shuvalov, M.A., ed., *Teatr komedii (al'bom)*, L., 1964.

Shvarts, E., 'Fantaziya i real'nost' (Iz arkhiva Evgeniya Shvartsa)', ed. by S. Tsimbal, *Voprosy literatury*, 1967, no. 9, 158-81.

Shvarts, E., 'Iz perepiski Evgeniya Shvartsa', published in *Voprosy literatury*, 1977, no. 6, 217-32.

Shvarts, E., *Kukol'nyi gorod. P'esy*, introduction by S. Dreiden, L., 1959.

Shvarts, E., *P'esy*, L., 1960.

Shvarts, E., *P'esy*, L., 1962.

Shvarts, E., *P'esy*, L., 1972.

Shvarts, E., *Povest' o molodykh suprugakh*, afterword by N. Akimov, M., 1958.

Shvarts, E., 'Priklyucheniya Gogenshtaufena', *Zvezda*, 1934, no. 11, 43-88.

Shvarts, E., 'Ten'', *Literaturnyi sovremennik*, 1940, no. 3, 3-62.

Shvarts, E., *Ten' i drugie p'esy*, L., 1956.

Shvarts, E., *Three Plays*, see under Pyman.

Shvarts, e., 'Tri chuda', *Neva*, 1955, no. 2, 167-9.

Shvarts, E., 'V dni ispytanii (iz dnevnika E.L. Shvartsa)',

in *Vstrechi s proshlym (sbornik neopublikovannykh materialov TsGALI SSSR)*, Book 1, M., 1972, 228-34.

'Skazka dlya vzroslykh', *Literaturnyi sovremennik*, 1940, no. 5-6, 228-9.

Smirnova, V., 'Skazochnik na teatre', in her *Sovremennyi portret*, M., 1964, 241-81.

Solov'eva, I., 'Dvinutsya da'lshe vpered', *Sovetskaya Rossiya*, 4 October 1956, 3.

Sotsialisticheskii realizm i khudozhestvennoe razvitie chelovechestva, ed. N.K. Gei and others, M., 1966.

Tairov, A., 'Mayakovskii na stsene', *Teatr*, 1940, no. 12, 60-3.

Tsimbal, S., 'Evgenii L'vovich Shvarts (K 60-letiyu so dnya rozhdeniya)', in *Voprosy detskoi literatury*, M., 1955, 415-16.

Tsimbal, S., *Evgenii Shvarts*, L., 1961.

Tsimbal, S., 'Evgenii Shvarts i ego skazki dlya teatra', in *Ten' (K postanovke p'esy v Leningradskom gosudarstvennom Teatre komedii)*, L., 1940, 3-15.

Tsimbal, S., *Evgenii Shvarts: kritiko-biograficheskii ocherk*, L., 1961.

Tsimbal, S., 'Kainovo tsarstvo', *Iskusstvo kino*, 1963, no. 8, 79-81.

Tsimbal, S., 'Mudraya predannost' teatru', *Teatr*, 1969, no. 4, 42-9.

Tsimbal, S., 'Poiski komedii', *Literaturnaya gazeta*, 10 May 1940.

Viner, A., *'Ten''*, *Teatr*, 1961, no. 3, 105-7.

Vladimirov, S.V., ed., *Ocherki istorii russkoi sovetskoi dramaturgii*, vol. III, 1945-1967, L., 1968.

Vladimirov, S.V. and G.A. Lapkina, eds., *Ocherki istorii russkoi sovetskoi dramaturgii*, vol. II, 1934-1945, L., 1966.

Yankovskii, M., 'Detskaya dramaturgiya Leningrada', *Teatr i dramaturgiya*, 1936, no. 9, 534-9.

Yankovskii, M., 'Fantaziya i deistvitel'nost'. O tvorchestve Evg. Shvartsa', *Iskusstvo i zhizn'*, 1940, no. 2, 13-15.

Yankovskii, M., *Leningradskii Teatr komedii*, L., 1968.

Zagorskii, M., 'Spektakli Teatra komedii', *Vechernyaya Moskva*, 4 August 1944, 3.

Zalesskii, V., 'Na lozhnom puti (Zametki o Leningradskom teatre komedii)', *Teatr*, 1949, no. 8, 40-9.

Zalesskii, V., '*Ten*'. Spektakl' Teatra komedii', *Trud*, 26 May 1940.

'Zayavki i p'esy', *Rabochii i teatr*, 1936, no. 3, 31-2.

Zharov, M., '*Obyknovennoe chudo*', *Sovetskaya kul'tura*, 22 May 1956, 2.

Zhdanov, N., 'O poetike komicheskogo', *Teatr*, 1940, no. 7, 95-101.

Zhezhelenko, M., 'Akimov', in *Portrety rezhisserov*, book 1, M., 1972, 55-96.

Zograf, N.G. and others, eds., *Ocherki istorii russkogo sovetskogo dramaticheskogo teatra*, I, 1917-1934, M., 1954; II, 1935-1945, M., 1960.

Zolotnitskii, D., 'Zaboty komedii', *Neva*, 1962, no. 9, 189-99.